New Ways of Teaching
in the Church School

The Ladder

of Learning

BY VICTOR HOAG

Greenwich · Connecticut ·

Second Printing

© 1960 by The Seabury Press, Incorporated
Library of Congress Catalog Card Number: 60-11085
332-162-Mu-3.5-2
Printed in the United States of America

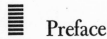 Preface

THERE ARE hundreds of fine teachers throughout the Church, but not enough of them. There are too many who are half-hearted, or frustrated, or about ready to quit. And many devoted teachers are plodding along, year after year, in set ways, unaware of how much more joyous and effective their teaching would be if they could try the new devices. Outside the Sunday schools there are hosts of fine Christians who would really like to help children, but do not know how to start.

Nearly everyone realizes that great advances have been made in educational theory and practice in both the secular and the religious fields. Many who feel that they would like to know the new ways would like to have them stated simply. Others, feeling threatened by the new, are critical and on the defensive. They do not accept the newer plans mainly because they do not realize how much the old have failed. This was what first opened the eyes of religious-education leaders —the discovery of the deplorable lack of positive results from our old-line Sunday schools. Chaplains in the Army and Navy and at colleges were appalled at the lack of both knowledge and interest discovered in the young people who were the products of average parishes. The informed and practicing churchman was a rarity.

There is no one best way to teach, but there are in use today many inadequate ways of teaching which should be recognized and corrected. And there are many new and delightful ways which can readily be learned. How can we show the contrast? It is almost universally true that teachers never see other teachers in action. Like preachers who never hear sermons because they must be in their own pulpit every Sunday morning, so teachers must always be with their classes. If you could only see some fine teacher using the new methods! If you might sit (unobserved and taking notes) through one whole session with a star teacher using the new approach, you would soon feel that you could do the same. If you could talk with the teacher, hear what he or she is aiming at, and later discuss the whole problem in your parish teachers' meeting, you would soon be trying the same things in your class.

This may not easily be arranged in the ordinary parish where there are few, if any, teachers using the new ideas. Sometimes one model class in a parish will serve to illustrate. Teachers learn by visiting this class. Well-planned teachers' meetings can provide demonstrations. Movies of real classes are now available. The reading of this book should help. Teaching improves when the whole educational awareness of a parish is raised.

In spite of many guides, introductions, and handbooks, teachers tend to reproduce in their classrooms the kind of teaching on which they were raised. This has been going on for generations without our being aware of it. In spite of some efforts by the seminaries in recent years, our young clergy are on the whole conservative and traditional in their attitude toward the religious education of children. This may be an inevitable result of the necessary amount of time spent in the seminary in drilling on the vast accumulation of the *content*—the lore, formulas, literature, cultus, and history of Christianity.

This is our first problem: to get our clergy and other teachers to realize that there are all sorts of other ways, and to try them out. Because the reader may feel prejudiced toward the new theory and resist it, we have placed the practical and inspirational sections at the start. These are: "The Teacher as a Person," "The Knack of Teaching," and "Group Life."

After reading some of the chapters that describe the new methods in application in the class, you may wish to understand the philosophy behind these delightful and vital ways. This is given in Part IV, "The New Objectives."

This is a book for skimming and skipping about in. It has no suspenseful plot developing from the first to the last pages. Its only aim is to capture the interest of the novice teacher and to get him to read—actually read—some bits that appeal—with the hope that through him better ways will begin to seep into his parish. Try out a single suggestion, then others. By all means seek other sources of information about them.

After all, you must teach in your own way, in spite of texts and guides. This point, indeed, is one of the fundamentals of the newer ways: that you bring to the "teaching moment," to *your* class, to these particular children, on *this* Sunday morning your very best—not a canned talk, but a living touch. Only life can start life.

This book is based on material that has appeared in *The Living Church* in my column "Talks with Teachers." Its main argument is: A new day has come in religious education; you can take part in it if you will. In the betrothal in the marriage service, the bride and groom each say firmly: "I will." This is the will-to-love. There is a will-to-teach evident in all devoted teachers; but it is present (though dormant) in every earnest Christian. To stir this latent motive is the purpose of this book.

VICTOR HOAG

Contents

PART I

The Teacher as a Person

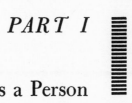

1

Starting with You

WITH ALL the talk about our dealing with *persons*, rather than things, subjects, or methods, it is well that we pause and consider the teacher as a person. In the fall, when church schools are starting up all over the land, many teachers, old and new, will be meeting their classes for the first time. The first session, by general agreement, is to be spent on some form of "getting acquainted"—names, families, addresses, and such. Then comes the comparing of summer experiences, to start the habit of sharing. Later, if the teacher is wise, he will make notes on each child so that his knowledge of their real lives deepens all through the year.

To these children, real persons, we are to address our efforts. It is our mission this year to teach *them*, not some shadowy ideal or typical children. They may be found to include the whole range of the four soils encountered by the sower in the parable—hard (unretentive), shallow (superficial), weedy (confused, cluttered), and good. Gradually we make ourselves remember, as we prepare and teach each lesson, that all that each child is, all he has been through, comes with him into class each Sunday morning.

And this is equally true of the teacher—every teacher. Each is a person who has come thus far on his immortal way through experiences both good and bad. He is the product of what has happened to him. To appreciate this is a proper responsibility of the leader of the school. Conceivably the rector keeps a growing record of the background and abilities of each teacher. Or at least he carries this information in his head, so that he can make allowances for each individual: this teacher is adaptable; that one, limited but devoted; another can handle the new courses; some may never be able to do so.

Teachers themselves can be aware of their own capacities and limitations. New teachers who are taking a class for the first time this fall may be mainly conscious of their textbook, which they have been studying earnestly. They might well study themselves, to see what they have to offer. A little meditation might start with the following points:

What do I know? Not much about the Bible, that's sure. And some assorted bits of lore about the Church. Yet, as I teach I can increase this knowledge through the year. I can look up every point that arises in class. And I will call on the rector as a resource person, always at hand.

Why am I teaching? Just what really are my motives? Was it just to please the rector? Do I have any interest in the lives of people—of my pupils? Do I tie my teaching up with my personal religion and a sense of mission? If I am doing this (partly) for the satisfaction of power over youth or of breaking a record or of dogged habit, can I enrich these motives by deepened devotion?

What is my idea of education—and particularly of religious education? Is it to hand out traditional information, to instill a code of behavior, or to guide growth in the Christian fellowship? What do I hope to accomplish? Or is all this hazy and unformed in my mind? (Most of this book is written to help you clarify your ideas of Christian education.)

What enthusiasms do I have which I would like to give

to my children? Music? Vestments? Intercession? Dramatics? Mission study?

What skills can I share? Drawing? Handicrafts? Singing? Modeling? Creative writing?

But deeper than all these, more important in teaching the Faith, there is your life of worship, whatever it may be. Can you commend, from personal practice, not only evening but morning prayers? Regular communions? Daily Bible reading, meditation? These are your best offerings to your class.

What *you are* will speak through your teaching. All that you believe and practice will somehow be communicated to your children. The remark of a small child about one of his companions illustrates this. He said: "I don't think Johnnie ever *thinks* about God." If one child can notice this lack in another, what will he detect in you?

For all you are or are not, you have enough to start with. You, like your pupils, are in mid-course, growing. It is your privilege to strive earnestly this year to grow with them.

2

How Jesus Taught

Jesus seems to have taught by beginning with what people knew already, asking their opinions, and then pointing to some great truth. His use of parables, although much noticed, is really secondary to this. *He started with people's present knowledge.*

A vivid lesson may be learned from a close study of a single incident in His ministry—the walk with the two disciples on the Emmaus road. Note the steps closely.

First, He came where they were. He caught up with them as they walked along on their journey, disillusioned and despairing men, and fell into step with them. At once they accepted Him as a companion of the road and allowed Him to join their conversation.

They did not recognize Him. No doubt this was the Lord's intention: human contact now; they would discover Him later. (Mary had not recognized Him in the garden; neither did the fishing disciples on the shore. Did He disguise Himself, or were they not quite ready to accept Him glorified and triumphant?)

Next He asked them: "What are you talking about? You seem so sad." They were surprised that He did not know the terrible news from Jerusalem. But He insisted that they tell Him all the details and their opinions and feelings about them. He wanted them to put it into their own words.

Then He added something. He spoke confidently of the problem of the Messiah and gave quantities of detailed citations from the Bible to prove that the incidents actually fitted the expectations of the prophets. He was acting as a resource person, adding to their store of knowledge. But He was also giving *meaning* to the whole sequence. Still they did not know Him.

The long walk over, He arranged that *they* should invite Him to sup with them. And then, in the act of relationship which He had so recently taught them—in the breaking of the bread—it happened! They knew Him. And in the instant they were left to themselves.

That is not the end of the teaching. Driven by their discovery, they sought the Church, the inner fellowship. They rushed back the seven miles to the city and burst into the upper room, sharing their joy. As they ran, they recalled the excitement they had felt while they were being taught.

Now trace this same sequence in a well-planned and well-taught church-school class: The teacher began by mentioning an accident that had happened in the neighborhood during the week. A child had been seriously injured by a car driven by a youth too young to have a driver's license. The children were all talking about it, and the teacher let them talk. After the details she began to ask for their opinions.

"Whose fault was it—the child's, the boy's, or his parents'?" "Could the law stop such things?" And so on, reaching for meanings. And then the deeper levels: "Did God have anything to do with this?" "What is God's plan for our lives?" "Does God permit accidents?" "What can we do when something happens to us?"

Still the teacher was a companion, not felt to be teaching. The children were merely thinking through a slice from life.

Then the inner question: "If the little boy dies, how can

we explain it?" This led at last to the simple statement that Jesus was killed—though He was good and did not deserve it. But God must have had a great reason.

The session turned out to be on the Christian duty of caring for those in trouble. There were found (toward the end of the session) some Bible passages. One was about the healing of the nobleman's son.

And then—the children were talking about Jesus and His care and love. The teacher was forgotten. And one child said (though perhaps the teacher planted the idea), "Couldn't we go up in front of the altar and pray for the child?"

They were the Church. They had been led to their Lord, and they acted as brethren. And I thought of the well-known concluding words of Albert Schweitzer's *Quest of the Historical Jesus:*

He comes to us, as of old by the lakeside He came to those men who knew Him not. He speaks to us in the same words, "Follow Me!" And sets us to the tasks which He has to fulfill for our time. He commands, and for those who obey Him, whether they be wise or simple, He will reveal Himself in the toils, the conflicts, the sufferings which they shall pass through in His fellowship. And as an ineffable mystery they shall learn in their own experience who He is.*

* Albert Schweitzer, *Quest of the Historical Jesus* (New York: Macmillan, 1954). Quoted with permission.

3

Preparing Your Lesson

FOR THE church school teacher every Sunday is a fresh start, a separate and new problem. Although the course is in progress and each Sunday the children are the same, each meeting requires careful preparation. While the present style of teaching is fluid and continuous, we can never be sure that the interest of the previous Sunday (after the seven-day gap, during which many engrossing thoughts have occupied the minds of everyone, pupils and teacher) will carry over. You may plan to use this interest. But if it does not strike fire, then the teacher must be prepared to provide the new idea, the fresh push, that will make the new session profitable.

Each week, then, you must have a plan, some new material, and be ready to give some real guidance as well as to utilize the bubbling energies of your pupils. *Every week you must prepare your lesson.* How to do this can be as personal as any creative act, for it is as a person that every teacher faces his pupils and labors to help them learn their religion.

Looking over the written lesson outlines of many teachers, the writer has been impressed by the wide variety of plans, aims, and materials revealed. No two teachers—especially the best teachers—make their outlines the same, even though they may be using the same basic textbook. This is so for many obvious reasons. Their classes may differ in the intelligence, development, and grouping of their pupils. They may decide to spend more time on one theme than another.

In spite of this general situation, there should be a fairly uniform scheme which will form the skeleton outline of every lesson plan. If a teacher has this in mind, it might make it a little easier, in the press of weekly duties, to start and finish his planning without too much strain.

The following is a general, rule-of-thumb procedure which, once you have it in your head, will expedite your weekly preparation.

Preliminaries. Pray. Visualize your little circle. Pray for each one, name by name. See their faces. Think. Face your problem: how much time will I have? Recall what happened last Sunday, on recent Sundays. Look over your notes, jotted down just after last week's session. (If you are blessed with an observer, you will have had a conference with him or her. Perhaps you now have the observer's notes in hand—about the session as a whole and a few notes added for each child's case.)

Review of year's theme. Are we still on our assigned subject? This was given to you in your teacher's guide, or by the parish authorities, as your area in the total curriculum, and you are expected to have it in mind all through the year. You may have to wander from it, as the interests and accomplishments of the class take over some Sundays; but if you entirely ignore your main theme, going off on some tangents of your own, and come out in June with very little taught, you are not doing your duty. You are part of a great program, and the authority you exercise in your class is delegated to you by the Church. This review may not take long. The next step is more difficult.

Purpose of this lesson. Write out in your own words what you think should be the reason for this coming lesson. This should be in one or two sentences. You will read what you wrote for last Sunday's aim, and decide whether to repeat or stress this in another way or to take a new direction. Ask yourself: "What great truth, doctrine, experience, or reality of the Christian faith do I want them to appreciate (or start to appreciate) this time?" (Remember, it's for *them*—just that little circle of children whom you know so well. This is not going to be just your own self-expression, nor yet a copying of the printed heading in your guide. What do *they need?*)

Once you have decided on and phrased this purpose to your satisfaction, the rest follows. You are not going to read your statement to anyone. It is to help you clarify your thoughts and aim your planning. You will look at it again, as you prepare the following Sunday's lesson, to see how nearly it worked out.

Opening moments. Decide just what will happen first. Shall it be the roll call (it is usually a waste of time and spoils the approach)? Or shall it be a short drill or other activity to cover up the disturbance from the tardy ones from the choir? In particular, what shall be the *opening words?* These are to be aimed at starting that solid block of purposeful conversation which will lead into the substance of this lesson. This will require some real thinking. Write out several questions that will call for opinions and reactions. Try to put in some element of debate. You may tell, for example, an open-end story, calling on the children to discuss and decide. Or read a short Bible passage requiring their reaction. Or have them write on a slip of paper: "What I am afraid of"—"What I want most"—"What I like about my home"—"How I help (tasks) in our home."

Steps in your teaching. This is your real "lesson plan"— possible stages through which you hope to steer the conversation. If, for example, you have decided on a "lore lesson" (subject matter), determine the method or means for presenting this—by telling a story, silent reading from Bible or

Prayer Book, a drill, a game, a visit, etc. Sometimes this plan will contain a number of items of things to do, sometimes a definite sequence of *ideas* to be developed.*

Activity. There should be something to do after a definitely ended period of talk or study. This can be handwork, marching, finger games, acting, even singing. It may be the showing of a filmstrip, with the required change of seating and attention. For older pupils it can be writing, research, a role play, or a skit. But plan something, as well as an alternative. And have all needed materials and equipment ready and in place before the class starts.

In your planning you will try to select an activity that in some way may serve as an expression of what you are teaching. You might ask yourself: "Shall I have them crayon another of those printed outlines the publisher has provided? Or shall I try them on freehand drawing?"

Closing. Try to allow enough time for this. The final minutes may be for memory drill, planning coming events, reviewing, saying the class prayer. You may ask older pupils to evaluate: "What did we learn?"

There you have it, your usual steps in preparing your lesson. Boiled down these are: preliminaries, year's theme, purpose of this lesson, opening moments, steps, activity, closing.

You can work in many variations. You will need helps, and you are beginning to know where to look for them. Each week, then, your plan of attack—*written down*—in hand. Without it you will be fumbling—yes, bluffing. With it you will be master of the situation.

* See "Lore and Concern" for the four different types of lesson.

4

Authoritarian or Permissive

WATCHING THE little needle on the control panel of a delicate machine, the operator can gauge accurately the response of the machinery and can control its speed and intake. Perhaps you have wondered if such a gauge could be invented for measuring the movement of a class. What would it tell? Could it reveal the thrusts, the overloads, the smooth periods of full capacity, the danger signs, the loose connections, the different kinds of behavior?

Let's imagine that such a delicate indicator has been invented and that it is connected with your class. You might keep an eye on it. Or a supervisor might watch it, take notes, and discuss points later. Our delicate needle, let us say, is geared to respond instantly to two opposite or alternating forces. These forces are always operating, in some manner, in every class session. They are the thrusts of authoritarianism and permissiveness. On the far left side of our gauge is marked the letter A, and on the right, the letter P. Between these extremes our delicate needle is in constant motion.

Below are given, in contrasted pairs of words, some of the forms of tension between these two forces.

Key Words of Authoritarianism	Key Words of Permissiveness
TEACHER is responsible for the whole program of the class. May dominate, from both temperament and habitual methods.	PUPILS feel it is their class, want to do things their own way, resent too much repression. They have minds and ideas of their own.
AUTHORITY is given to the teacher, who feels he must dominate, control the teaching situation. His will must prevail. He must never "lose control."	FREEDOM is the style of all alert persons, especially healthy children. They want to do without restraints. They are not rude —just very much alive.
MUST, says the teacher unsure of himself, dependent on his teacher status.	MAY I, says the pupil, yearning for recognition as a person.
DISCIPLINE is the avowed duty of the strict teacher, who feels that solid purpose and fixed goals are necessary if there is to be any "schooling."	SELF-CONTROL, found in all well-developed democratic groups, is the secret yearning of those under restraint. It will develop if expected and permitted.
CONTENT of books, the tradition, the "things they ought to be taught," is the chief concern of this teacher.	CONTACT with people, ideas, places, experiences are the felt needs of lively pupils, though they may not know how to say this.
TYRANNY becomes the dominant tone of any class in	LICENSE, leading to rebellion or withdrawal, may be-

14

Key Words of Authoritarianism	*Key Words of Permissiveness*
which the teacher pushes his authority too far and constantly. (The needle seems stuck at the left.)	come the desire of pupils too long kept under external control. Outbreaks of disorder may arise from bored listeners. We avoid this extreme by proper permissiveness.

The truth is, either extreme of the needle represents a breakdown in the smooth workings of the educational machine. The two thrusts, the constant interplay of these vital forces of pupil versus teacher, must be harmonized. Both are persons, both able (unless the strain reaches the breaking point) to make adjustments to the other. Both need the other's vital urges and find the satisfaction of success only in a poised relationship.

Pupils need discipline of a sort and feel lost without it—but discipline based on the gracious words of permissiveness. The teacher must count on vigor and push from his class, for without it there would be no response, no originality—indeed, no learning. Just how loosely can he hold the reins?

In all this we are at the heart of the contrast between the old ways of teaching and the new.

In the ideal classroom the needle is forever alive. It vibrates back and forth as the teacher briefly acts his part of authority, then permits the vigorous response of the pupils. What does the needle tell about your class?

5

Jack-of-All-Trades

"Do you expect me to pick up after class is over?" a teacher objected, while complaining to the rector that certain of her materials had been lost during the week. "Doesn't the janitor take care of things?"

"I'm afraid not," replied the rector. "You will have to realize that whatever happens in your classroom is your responsibility, and you cannot count on others to help."

Picking up is one of the many things expected of a church teacher. Let's decide this. Frankly, if you don't see that your things are put away before leaving on Sunday, just who will do it, and when? Is there someone in your home who picks up after you, as they once did when you were a little child? The appearance of some classrooms when the teacher has left is appalling. Can this lack of system have any relation to the fact that this teacher is having trouble with discipline, not knowing the elementary tricks of assigning duties, both as an outlet for energy and a training in responsibility?

But there are other functions belonging to the teacher which may not, at first thought, be considered part of teaching. The wonderful teacher is many-sided and must take on many characters in the course of a single morning. Like the old-fashioned hired girl (genus now extinct), she is expected to be willing and able to do anything that needs to be done.

Just to be sure you new teachers know what is really expected of you, we give this list. The perfect teacher is an:

Inventor. Necessity is the mother of invention, and there is always necessity and urgency about teaching. You may have to solve almost anything in a moment, in the twinkling of an eye. Are they too slow at their writing? You devise true-false questions or take a page from a workbook. Is there no table space in your crowded room? You find lap-boards. Does paste dry or get all over pupils? You discover the office stapler, clean and neat. Do they lack interest in memorizing? You devise a new game. Is the story in the book too short, too inane? You improve on it or invent another.

Housekeeper. Your room is the home of your class, and you are the housemother. Part of the class morale is to be proud of the way they do things, including tidiness and respect for others. Could the room be improved by curtains, paint, shades, shelves? The housekeeper plans and gets things done.

Janitor. Yes, it's a shame, but chairs are never right. Each Sunday no one but you can check, make certain they are arranged in just the right way for this day's lesson plan. And when chairs are wobbly or broken, you fix them—or contrive to have the repairs made. Wishing and grumbling is not enough.

Memory expert. Do you really know their names, homes, ages, whether they are baptized, confirmed? From church families or not? The names and interests of their parents? Their schools, problems, and hobbies? Your class roll is, of course, always near, but do you have these things on your mind? Do you remember assignments, committees, stories, promises?

Playwright, author, and impresario. The script (your lesson outliné) you prepared on Saturday is for your special class.

You alone know their abilities and needs, the stars and bit-players.

Actor. Do you resent it if we say you must "put on an act?" Yet all successful social conduct calls for "setting your face," being something more than your inclination suggests. Your voice must be controlled, your poise dynamic, your charm turned on. For the short while of your scene you try to fill the role assigned you: the perfect teacher.

And so the rest: musician, poet, minister, scholar, package-wrapper, sign-painter, artist, coach, and friend. That is why teachers grow by teaching. That is what is meant by saying: "Give them all you've got."

6

Resources Unlimited

SHE HAD said: "There isn't enough material in my textbook. It gives me a few ideas, but my lessons are thin. I often run out of material before the bell rings. Where can I find things to enrich my lesson?"

Her rector had replied: "But there are materials right in your book which you have overlooked. Here, turn to page six, in the introduction. Did you notice this heading, 'Resources'?"

The teacher admitted that she had overlooked this because she was in a hurry to teach the first lesson. Now, together, they went over the page. Here were mentioned several books, a published report, and some filmstrips.

"Where can I get these?" the teacher asked, and her rector replied: "We have them or will get them for you."

By "resources" we mean teaching helps, specific or intangible, which will give variety, interest, enrichment, depth, and increased pleasure to the class experience. These must be at hand, even *in* hand, truly available to the teacher. The editors of every course have these in mind and list a few. Then when the parish authority hands a teacher the textbook, the teacher should be told: "In the parish supply cabinet you will find all the aids checked in the introduction. Just ask the secretary for them."

There is a wide variety of resources available, and teachers should be encouraged to ask for them. Many parishes make it needlessly difficult for their teachers or ignore and neglect this matter entirely.

"Certainly. We'll get you anything you wish, within reason. Just tell the superintendent or the secretary." But few teachers ever do. Why? Because our untrained teachers are text-bound and have not been taught to recognize their responsibility for seeking out and using extra material.

Good teaching brings to the experience of the class a rich variety of teaching aids; it is the teacher's job to locate and employ these aids.

Just what kinds of resources are available and where shall we look for them?

(1) Books. Some will deal with the subject area of the course; some will give techniques of applicable methods—for example, finger games, handwork, choral reading, role playing, and dramatization.

(2) Filmstrips, of which every parish should maintain a growing library.

(3) Pamphlets, tracts, and brochures, often from sources not well-known, but discovered by the editor.

(4) Publications of the Church's National Council and of diocesan and provincial units.

(5) People in the parish with special knowledge or skills—for advice or as visitors to the class.

(6) Things brought by the pupils: interest objects, treasures, pictures, old books.

(7) The parish church, its appointments, personnel, services, and life in general. You frequently use these by reference to them, a visit, or class participation.

(8) Church magazines. Of course you subscribe to at least one—preferably a weekly. If you do not, your school might be moved to subscribe for you—as a slight reward, but mainly as a working tool.

(9) The treasures of your own mind. What are all the experiences, thoughts, and achievements of your whole life but a bank, your storehouse of memory, more readily available than you realize?

So you prepare your lesson. First, you digest the short plan in your text. Then you dress it up with plans for allusions, activities, questions. For these you begin to search among your resources.

What can I find to make this point come alive? What book will enrich the background of my story? Perhaps Edersheim for life and scenes in Palestine. Perhaps a picture or a filmstrip. What problem from life can I find or invent that will provoke discussion, compel decision? What suggestion in our teachers magazine can I try out?

So, like the good householder, you draw out of your treasures things new and old. As you gradually learn to do this, you will increasingly deserve to be known as a resourceful person.

7

In Praise of Ingenuity

IF WE were asked to list the many good qualities necessary in a successful teacher, no doubt spiritual devotion and zeal would be placed at the top. Along with this we might demand that characteristic of self-motivating, self-starting desire, of aroused interest which makes a teacher a center of enthusiasm and a fountain of life. A teacher must be vital. To this quality of original energy, we must add the balancing requirement of dogged determination, steady faithfulness.

But high in the list I place ingenuity—the quality of meeting a situation and using whatever means you have at hand. Robinson Crusoe (or rather, Daniel Defoe) was ingenious. Too often perhaps the author sent his hero back to the wrecked ship to find the basic materials—miraculously convenient—necessary for his projects. But on the whole Crusoe made use of the tools and materials he found, adapting them by his own labor and skill. Often he had to learn a new procedure to meet a need. He was master of his peculiar situation. He not only survived under far from standard conditions, but he made life safe and even luxurious.

Anybody can go to a well-stocked school store and bring back a package of expensive supplies. It takes little originality to follow the explicit instructions of some teachers' handbooks. But the creative artist, the real leader, uses what he has on hand. He decides what must be done, and does it—usually with makeshift materials.

Some teachers want a guide in which the procedures, step by step, are all worked out by an editor. They faithfully digest the directions under such headings as "Opening Moments," "Equipment to Be Secured in Advance," "The Story," "Illustrative Anecdotes," "Points for Discussion," and finally "Handwork and Projects." Such carefully prepared helps are not to be disparaged. But the frame of mind that requires them all the time and looks upon teaching as the obedient following of the orders of an impersonal textbook, is not the highest and most effective for teaching. We do need some over-all steering, if only to keep proportion in the year's planning and to avoid spending too much time on one unit. But such helps must fit your case, or your teaching will not sparkle. In the hands of a dull teacher they tend to accentuate the dullness.

Live teachers know that there are no two classes alike, that situations change and require fresh approaches, new devices. It is true that you can make the suggestions of others your own, and in the wealth of ideas you will find several to stimulate your own inventiveness. Picking up the bright ideas of others is the work of any clever leader. Yet there is no substitute for originality in methods. We say "in methods" because if you are entirely original in basic *religious* ideas, you will probably be heretical.

The better guides give just enough information to stimulate you to your own original adaptation. Or they hand on an assortment of tips, suggestions, and tested projects—like a well-filled refrigerator—for you to nibble on and digest. This. kind of guide reiterates the refrain of this book: a teacher is a person and must personalize all his material.

Printed guides, however, usually run to three types. The first type is a complete instruction manual, with every move anticipated and described. The second or obvious type is one which tells what everybody knows how to do anyway, like a recipe for boiling potatoes. This is usually the product of a tedious and plodding editor who will not trust anyone to be original. The third type of guide is likely to be very short, often exasperating in its effort to throw all creative responsibility on the teacher.

But, with or without benefit of printed guide, the inventive teacher is the happy man. He sees problems, things to be done, before materials and methods traditionally prescribed. Here are some common problems calling for ingenuity and demanding some solution: how to interest the slower-witted members of the class; how to get home assignments done; how to induce originality in writing; noisy classrooms; new materials for handwork; suitable service projects.

When you see in classrooms evidences of new things being done, common materials used in a new way, you may be sure that here happy teaching is going forward and that the class is blessed with an ingenious teacher.

8

Hands Off!

"LET ME show you how to do it," says the father to his small son who is nailing some wheels on a box. A better wagon is the result, but the boy has stopped playing with it and is doing something else.

"Kids don't stick to anything long," remarks the parent sagely. "See, he has lost interest already."

How can we show this father the truth? That he has killed the boy's imaginative project by taking it over; that the boy, who has inherited the sensitive creative impulses of his father, instinctively resents adult interference.

This is a truth of all dynamic education: experimental life must not be thwarted by too much supervision. The lesson that parents and teachers—all who deal with unfolding life— must learn is never to interfere with an original activity while it is in progress. The exception would be only where the work was dangerous or destructive.

Most otherwise-splendid teachers have a blind spot here. They cannot realize that "showing them how to do it" is not their duty. Their part, rather, is to get them started, to lead them somehow to want to do, to make, to draw, to act, to sing. *The only time a teacher should help a pupil in his handwork is when the pupil asks for it.* And then the teacher should not insist on her own methods, but merely help the pupil overcome his difficulty. The problem is to keep him producing happily, to prevent his getting discouraged. It is the pupil's work, not the teacher's.

It is not easy for anyone of any age to start and finish a creative work of art. Think how hard it is for you, even when you have paper and pencils ready, to decide *what* to draw. And then, once an idea forms and you have begun to work on it, how you resent any volunteer critic's suggestions.

"Let me alone!" you say inwardly. "It's my own idea, and I want to work it out in my own way. I'm busy. I'm just getting the feel of this. I wish you'd go away!"

Such a sense of annoyance must be vaguely felt by the child, in the midst of a creative act, when an adult interferes and tries to tell him a better way. In part, it is an intrusion upon his stream of thought. Partly it is felt as a criticism of himself and his enthusiasm. Possibly no one is so readily hurt and frustrated as when he is criticized while in the midst of an original and imaginative action. "Children at work at creative art" is the sign that should be hung over every class table. That means: "Keep your fat adult hands off!"

True, we are not to turn our Sunday session into an art school, nor yet a factory to manufacture identical articles by a set design. But we do realize now that it is important that every child have the opportunity to express himself through the arts. The art forms of acting, music, and drawing or painting are ready channels for the expression of religious feeling. Freedom, combined with self-discipline, is one of the Christian goals.

Good teachers no longer ask their pupils to crayon within the lines of a printed picture. Rather, following the discussing of the story, they provide them with large sheets of paper and plenty of watercolors or crayons. Beyond the mildest controls, the children are allowed to interpret the story they have just heard. They are neither hurried nor forced to do it. They do it because it is a pleasure and because on other Sundays they have found it a way of being themselves. They know that their work will be respected, not ridiculed.

This is no simple or slight matter. Many adults have undoubtedly been thwarted permanently in childhood at just this point by some well-meaning teacher.

Write in your notebook: "In all art work, be friendly, appreciative, suggestive. But keep your hands off. One touch may spoil the whole experience."

9

Coach, Quarterback, and Scorekeeper

THE NEW way of teaching has been aptly compared to a game of football. It has its goals, its team effort, the unpredictable movement of its plays, and the experience gained for the next game. While all the players are participants, certain persons have conspicuous parts. The coach knows the objectives, and he also knows each player. The quarterback calls the signals and runs each play. The scorekeeper summarizes, records, and reports the results.

In our great game of teaching, played on the gridiron of parish life, the teacher must play in turn the parts of coach, quarterback, and scorekeeper. As coach you are responsible for training and arranging your players (pupils), for creating morale, for providing equipment; but above all you must know the rules and objectives of the game.

The idea of knowing our goal is just now being questioned. "Certainly we are teaching *children*, but we must teach them *something*" is the common form of the complaint. This is saying that we, as thoughtful teachers, must know what we are trying to accomplish. It also says that the "something" had better be pretty definite. But to conservative educators this means largely that specific information shall be imparted and permanently lodged in every head. To a newer group the goal indeed includes some of the same incidental knowledge, but it also aims at learning the Christian life *now* by practicing it in community.

The coach knows that the object of the game is to get the ball over the goal line as many times as possible. So the teacher, accepting the responsibility of guiding his team, knows the job assigned to him. He may not make many high scores with this year's team, but at least he knows what he is working toward, and his men realize it, too. Just so our courses come to us from the editors with real goals set. Here is where many a teacher starts off wrong and never gets back on the field. He does not read the rules! He does not know the objective for the year. Look in the book!

Any printed text states its year's objective in the preface. Some authors are a little vague or wordy, but they know what the year is about, and no mistake. This you are to aim at from September to June. Sometimes the objective may be largely the learning of subject matter or the training in skills. Frequently there are several goals. Often it is the effort to reach a certain understanding, attitude, or change.

Here are some examples of annual goals, as stated in some of the current texts:

First Grade: "To bring about development in the child's attitude toward the Church . . . to create a deep conviction, from experience, that the Church is his home, too."

Fourth Grade: "That the Christian understanding of right and wrong be related to the growing conscience . . . which the nine-year-old is developing."

Seventh Grade: "To help pupils find the answers to their questions, Why should I believe . . . why obey . . . why go to church?"

A different series of texts gives these:

Second Grade: "To inspire the children to desire to accept our Lord's gracious invitation . . . to guide them along pathways which will take them into His Presence."

Sixth Grade: "To awaken each individual to the conscious-ness of God's purpose for his life . . . to make Christian choices . . . within the fellowship of the Church."

So the teacher as coach receives his over-all orders and plans the season's campaign. There are some forty games (Sunday-morning sessions) to be played.

Now you are on the team; now you are the quarterback, involved in the complicated business of advancing toward the goal. Each session of the class is a separate play. You work for variety.

That is why some teachers are baffled at first by the new courses. They are not used to calling the signals. They must learn that learning is done by active people together, with their own energies, relationships, and skills. They will dis-cover that the subject of religious education is the Christian life, lived in a real parish, in real families, and given meaning by discovering the relevance of the ancient Faith and its literature.

A teacher also must play the part of scorekeeper. After each play (session) he takes out his little notebook, with its page for each player on the squad, and notes the gains made by each, the mistakes, the score. This is evaluation, and it points to the next session. Follow up this gain, keep this interest rolling. (Today a new character has appeared—the *observer,* who takes over part of the duties of the scorekeeper, adding his judgment and help toward reaching the goal.)

Is the parable above too strained? We think not. We might even add that, although there is missing the roar of earthly applause, there is the unseen host of heaven, who are watch-ing us with eager prayers and who are singing the old school song of praise for those who have borne the burden and heat of the great game, and who on Home-coming Day will welcome us as worthy alumni.

PART II

The Knack of Teaching

10

Some Arts of Teaching

NEW TIMES call for new skills. Perhaps this is why older teachers seem at first baffled by the new-style courses. They are accustomed to the traditional fill-and-drill methods. Although familiar with some of the current devices, they have not used them very much. For example, the rule "work for response" may mean, to a teacher concerned mainly with subject matter, the giving-back of the substance of the lesson—in short, *recitation*. Methods employed for securing such response would be various forms of the drill, with frequent repetition and review.

Response, in the new emphasis, may include the methods above, but it also aims at providing a setting in which an *original* reaction will be produced by each pupil. The teaching skills required to secure this outcome will be quite diffent, as the aim is different.

No matter what the teacher's age, outlook, or experience, he must face the fact that the new goals are gradually being accepted and are being written into most of the recent textbooks. It is important, therefore, that all our teachers should be guided into understanding and using some of the new devices. These we like to call the *arts* of teaching. Here are five:

(1) *The art of guided group conversation and of democratic procedure.* Some people do this naturally, by a combination of innate respect for and courtesy toward other people's opinions, plus the social skill of controlling a group without seeming to be autocratic. Most people not conscious of the "group process"—that is, what may be happening when a number of people are talking together—seem at a loss as to how to cause this group energy to become profitable.

We cannot give it to you in a paragraph. The new group-life laboratories, where our leaders spend two solid weeks being trained in group methods, are creating hundreds of understanding teachers. The idea may be briefly and inadequately stated thus: We must live with people all our lives. Getting on with people, for their good and your own right development, calls for lifelong effort. Our lives have a bearing on other lives, some close to us, some more remote, and this is our call to do our "duty in the state of life unto which it shall please God to call" us—that is to say, the human circumstances and relations among which we find ourselves day by day. This is particularly true when the same group meet together habitually, such as a family or a Sunday-school class.

This first art means, more simply, that the teacher uses devices, opening statements, and class procedures that will help children learn *together*. For this the new texts give many excellent examples and clues, which the teacher will supplement.

(2) *The art of questioning for opinions.** It sounds easy, and it *is* easier than many think. If you want to know what a person thinks, why not ask him? What he is thinking is important to him and to you. If his idea is right, it will be a contribution to the class. If wrong, it will be aired and in time corrected by the influence of others.

The keys to this art lie in such leads as: "What did you

* See also "Questioning for Concerns."

34

think when . . ." and "Do you believe it is right to . . . ?" (giving a current situation calling for decision). And the clincher at the end of every argument: "Why do you think so?" This last may bring out reasons that may be sensible and feelings (buried emotions) that need airing and comparing.

(3) *The art of questioning for facts.* This was important in the past, and we must not scorn it now. Much information is acquired by our pupils and, to our surprise, retained. We must never fail to remember that we have to equip our children with the lore of their inheritance.

This requires that a certain quantity of information must be imparted and then reviewed and repeated frequently. The art called for here is in reality just the old practice of *drill.* Teachers may develop their own devices for this, but the heart of it lies in the teacher's own strong determination to equip his pupils with some permanent, accurate knowledge.

(4) *The art of discovering concerns and leading toward resources.* Our pupils are involved in a real world of people and ideas, all active and pressing. What is now impressing the pupils, or disturbing them, is the place where our teaching begins. This is much more than the starting "point of contact" of the older pedagogy. It is the living forefront of our people's lives. When we begin to know what is delighting or troubling them, we may helpfully lead them to the age-old resources of the Faith.

(5) *The art of listening.* This does not, of course, mean complete silence, but the willingness to wait patiently for replies. As we listen, with ears open for meanings and thoughts we had not expected, we shall begin to have a living "relationship" with our pupils. To get them to "say what you want them to say" is heavy adult dominance. To feel and to show that what each person says is important, leads to confidence and sympathetic sharing.

11

Necessary Techniques

COME, COME, let's not be fancy. "Technique" is just a campus word used to avoid the more earthy word "method." The dictionary adds that "technique refers to technical skill, especially in artistic work." Teaching religion is assuredly an art, calling out all the artist's originality, perception of life, and ingenuity. This is the elusive, the personal element. But every art and every artist develops necessary techniques which can be observed, shared, and copied (each in his own way) by other artists.

We need methods, then, to help us get away from the bungling and missing the mark which has been going on in our classrooms so long. If the lofty teachers seem to scorn methods, as if they were a substitute for reality, perhaps they are telling us something about their own sense of futility. They just haven't learned to use some good methods.

Here is the heart of the matter: methods are invented by workers to get something special done. Some methods come ready-made and can be gathered into working kits, like tools. Fishermen can buy many lures, but the best fishermen "study the fishes' curious ways" and frequently devise and tie their own flies. All teachers use some methods, but poor teachers use outmoded devices or repeat endlessly a single method.

Good methods are lively, with some element of fun or

pleasure. They should be varied; should call for participation; should be started swiftly, without undue lagging; should be used again if they work. They should employ skills already at least partially familiar to a child, and they should be designed to advance some desired purpose. Here is our clue: to get a certain thing accomplished. What do you wish might happen in your class this Sunday?

Various problems confront the teacher as he plans his next session or as he struggles in the midst of battle between the opening and closing bells. Here are some problems, listed not in their order of importance, nor completely, but to illustrate:

(1) *To forge the class into a real group*—sharing, accepting, helping, and learning from each other. There is no one method for this, except to use all the devices of sincere fellowship. The new texts give many, but you must make them your own.*

(2) *To discover real concerns and problems.* There are two general methods: One is to *ask* the children, and keep on asking and following up. The other is to give them ways of expressing themselves, as in written answers to the questions: "What do you want most?" "What are you most afraid of?" "What are you punished for?" And always the teacher's and observer's notebooks are building up details gleaned from each child's free remarks and actions.

(3) *To get things memorized.* Plenty of devices here—the large card, homework, recital in unison, contests. But always the will of the teacher to get it accomplished is needed, plus unfailing repetition and drill.

(4) *How to get them to do what you want them to do*—happily and on their own. Ah, here is the inner lock, opened only by the golden key of motivation. In a sense, this is the whole task of the teacher—to get pupils in motion. This is

* See the chapters in the following section, "Group Life."

the central nerve of leadership. You can learn if you keep trying. (But there is hidden poison here: a better plan may arise from the class instead of what you had decided.)

(5) *To secure less noise*—to have a courteous, self-disciplined class. Let the teacher talk less and more quietly. Try role playing, and notice how they listen attentively to their own kind. Or if the class has formed a pattern of violence, it may need a period of reorganization and frank talk leading to the setting up of some new ideals of class conduct.

(6) *To create interest in a new area.* Interest is in part familiarity. It takes time and many different new stages to build up. It calls for an opening note, repeated later and sounded in a variety of ways.

(7) *To get the shy, the unresponsive to speak.* Don't spend too much time on this. Such children will always be outtalked. Let them express themselves in other ways or just listen. But give them their chance now and then.

(8) *To prevent discussion from running too long.* That's easy. Plan some activity for the latter part of the period and switch to it on time. Most teachers let talk run too long because they have prepared nothing else.

(9) *To have the subject for today carry over into next Sunday.* This is the *result* of vital teaching; you won't need any technique for this.

12

Activities for Juniors

WE LEARN by doing far more than by being told. With children, who cannot listen very long, activity in the class is essential. The inventive, ingenious teacher thinks of plenty of things to do, has a stock of devices to give variety to the learning. There are recognized ways of securing participation which can be employed under even the limited conditions of the church school. Following are some activities suitable for pupils from the fifth grade up—that is, for children who can read and write and who have some manual skills.

(1) The most common and obvious form of activity, intended to involve every child, is the old-fashioned "reading 'round by verses." Each pupil has a Bible; all find the passage. The child on the teacher's left reads aloud the opening verse, the next child the next verse, and so on until the teacher stops them. Hundreds of teachers, knowing nothing better, use this as a kind of ritual every Sunday. (The grave temptation is that the teacher may use this to cover up his failure to prepare: he notes the passage listed at the top of the leaflet, starts the class reading 'round, and has decided what to make of it by the time the reading is completed. Such ad lib teaching is far more common than pastors realize.)

Some better forms of class Bible reading are these: (a) Each child must add, in his own words, some comment on the verse he has just read. (b) The teacher first presents the Bible material in his own words, then has the class read 'round for grasp of the Bible language. (c) Silent reading of verse or verses assigned; then ask a child to report to the class in his own words what he has read. Thorough teachers may even use the drama type of lesson by preparing in advance a list of the verses to be assigned to each child, fitting them to each one's known ability. Silent reading of short passages by the whole class is also a good method. (d) Partner reading, in which two pupils are assigned a short reading, then given time to confer and decide "the most important idea we found." The spokesman for each pair then reports to the class. (e) The same, with groups of two or three, but all groups reading the *same* passage. This is a simplified form of group Bible study, now in general use with adult classes.

(2) Compose a prayer. After a discussion of how prayers are constructed (the address, the character of God, the request or praise, and the ascription), provide pencils and paper and allow time for each child to write his own prayer. A suitable topic or reason for the prayer should first be agreed upon, such as thankfulness, help for a sick person, or the opening of a class session. "What could we put into such a prayer?" From the discussion ideas arise. It will surprise teachers how the most unlikely pupils will produce real prayers, and often a truly beautiful one is written. Frequently it requires several weeks to get the idea working. Many children like to try it at home and bring their written prayer to show the class. The using of the prayer by the class is part of this activity.

(3) After the story has been told, raise a question calling for reaction. "Do you think that Joseph should have told his brothers about his dreams?" Now we are getting some real self-expression, rather than the mere echoing of the teacher or book. "How do you feel about this? If you had been there, what would you have done?" Ask each in turn. If the ques-

tion does not bring ready response, try varying it. This is imaginative interpretation, and the teacher can provoke it more often than is usually the case.

(4) Write the story out in your own way. This should be done briefly, because of the limited time on Sundays. Other examples of original writing: a sentence a certain character might have spoken; adjectives describing a certain person; a list of all the hard words in the passage, or of all the persons mentioned.

(5) Draw a picture of the story. This is best if for some agreed purpose or place of display. But coloring in a printed or drawn outline is not drawing; it is simply stupid!

(6) Make something, for example, an illuminated prayer card, a bulletin board on which to post prayers in home prayer corners; place cards for a party at church; a crèche; a window transparency; a sand-table arrangement of some Bible story. (Every teacher should have a book on handwork.)

(7) Act the story out: (a) Paper-bag puppets are quick and easy and can be done around the class table. (b) Pantomime —action without words; later, dialogue is invented. (c) Tape-recording of spoken lines, and then have a silent dramatization of the story, while the dialogue is being played on the recorder (lots of fun). But any dramatization requires a private classroom, and who has one?

(8) Try role playing, a fairly new device. This means the quick, impromptu taking of parts—while seated—and inventing lines in character. Can be used to prepare for new experiences (like a trip), to interpret characters, or to reveal differing standards held by individual children. But this (or any dramatic attempt) requires some advance planning and discussion. (See the following chapter on role playing.)

(9) Make a poster. This involves a reason for showing it publicly, the selection of the words to put on it, the making, and finally the posting. Each step calls for decisions, division of duties, and group action.

(10) The search or research. A hunt for information or

somebody's opinion—an interview—to answer problems raised by discussion. It leads to the parish library or secures homework.

(11) The project—developed by using some of the methods above, and usually worked out over several sessions. It culminates in some public display and an evaluation—"What did we learn by doing this?"

Proposition: Activity teaching is not new; it belongs in all types of teaching, but is particularly appropriate and necessary with the new ways. It provides creative self-expression by which students make personal what would otherwise be only authoritarian handouts from the lips of an adult. It must not be mere busy work, the making of someone else's invented article. It must have some meaning that relates it to the lesson theme. Pupils should not all make the same article; if possible, permit each individual to design his own article. Large projects may be made or done jointly by all or by small groups of two or three.

Anything is an activity that is not passive listening to words spoken or read by the teacher.

13

Role Playing

THIS DELIGHTFUL form of expression is suitable for children in junior high school or older. It is simply impromptu dramatization in order to clarify an idea or experience. Its main purpose is to make a situation or problem seem real, and therefore easier to understand and discuss. By means of role playing a group can be helped to improve their sense of human relationships. Young people are very self-conscious and sensitive to what people think about them, and need to learn how people feel toward each other. A child is helped in this by taking the part of another person for a brief scene, inventing lines he would probably speak, and actually trying to understand that person's feelings by "being" him.

The steps in carrying out a role-playing period in class are simple, but must be understood by the teacher. The first time it is attempted the pupils may prove a little slow in getting the idea or hesitant about "acting," but in later sessions they will drop into it quickly with little coaching. First, the problem or scene is proposed. The teacher will have thought it out the first time, but later the class may come to a point in a discussion when someone proposes: "Let's play it out." After the scene is described and the relation of the characters is made clear, actors are appointed (or volunteers accepted) for each of the parts. At first two characters are enough; later, three. No setting or costumes are required. The actors merely move to one side, taking their chairs, and perform seated.

After the scene has run for about five minutes, the teacher says, "Cut!" This may be when the actors run out of lines and begin to repeat, but even if they don't, the scene will be brief. No outcome is to be reached; simply, the relation of the characters is to be established, and the actors are to "feel" their new roles.

Immediately the actors are asked to describe their sensations. They are addressed by their names in the play. "Mother, how did you feel when you told Johnnie he would lose his allowance this week?" "Johnnie, how did you feel when you told her about your failure in arithmetic?"

Then comes the discussion, for which the scene was only a prelude. The class discusses why each actor spoke as he did. At first, the specific scene is criticized. Sometimes there is a desire to do it over, and two different actors take the same parts. Later, as the discussion broadens, a general problem is raised. In this case it may be punishment, allowances, school subjects "you just can't get," truthfulness, or parents' understanding or lack of it.

Role playing is an intensely imaginative activity, appealing to young people and greatly useful in helping them to express themselves, as well as to understand the motives of others. They are growing in their social awareness and need sympathetic help in making their new adjustments. The teacher must be careful not to be critical or to make fun of any of the characters. Even the boy who clowns his part is to be taken seriously for the moment, since this is part of the junior-high behavior pattern, and it, too, is an outlet for feelings.

This device should be used with some caution by the teacher. As a rule, a child should not be asked to take a part similar to his own outstanding trait (for example, retiring, boisterous, teasing), since this only tends to set his characteristic. Again, it is unwise to set a scene for the deliberate purpose of showing up a misbehaving child by allowing the rest to say freely what they think of him. This will not be likely to change the trait and may produce only inward hurt and resistance. Let a pupil take a part different from his own personality—if possible, requiring the expression of an attitude that he needs to acquire—with the hope that he may grow into it. In any case, let them tackle the problem from the inside by living the part momentarily of one of the people in a particular situation.

The form above illustrates the acting-out of problems from a child's own world. Another possibility is the interpretation of Bible characters from a story that has just been told. "George, you be the servant who has just filled the water pots. Tell about it to the other servants. How did you feel?" Or: "How would one of the shepherds tell the story? You are a young shepherd. It is late Christmas Eve. You rush into the hut where the old shepherd is asleep. . . ."

Sometimes the role play may be done at the very end of the class period. The discussion is deferred until the following Sunday, when the children will come back with fresh ideas, perhaps arising from conversations at home.

When a class has learned to do this, they will readily ask to role-play an idea that has come up in the discussion. They will know that it is a direct way of "testing reality." This device should not be used all the time. It may be alternated with the open-end story, which is akin to it.

The formula or steps in making use of role playing may be listed as follows:

(1) Let the purpose of the teacher or the decision of the group define the general problem to be faced (for example, losing your temper, feeling neglected, property rights, being forgiving, prejudice).

(2) Invent a scene that illustrates this. Decide on a few

characters, give them names, and agree on their relation to each other (parent and child, clerk and customer, new and old pupil, etc.) and on the situation that causes them to meet and talk.

(3) Select the actors. Frequently this is done before the session to allow them a little time to think over their lines.

(4) Have characters take their places and begin at a word from the leader.

(5) Teacher or leader orders "Cut" before it drags.

(6) Actors are asked to state how they felt in the part.

(7) General discussion—first, of the scene acted and, then, of the larger issues involved. Sometimes the scene is done again by other actors to give a different interpretation. The discussion will often become heated and carry over to another session.

14

The Open-End Story

THIS DEVICE is an excellent one and, when understood and used correctly (and at the right moments), can stir depths of response unknown before. In brief, the open-end story is a tale from real life which stops before the outcome is reached, so that the hearers may discuss it and decide on its probable ending.

The device is not new, and we find authority for its use in the teachings of our Lord. His parables are samples of life— real life, known to His listeners—the ordinary situations of housekeeping, travel, farming, and politics of his times. We have frequently used His parables ineffectively. We have strained them into minute details, looking for hidden meanings and separating them from their living context.

For our Lord was nearly always speaking in public, and His sayings were heard and remembered in the midst of controversy. Not only was He heckled, but He encouraged discussion. Read your Gospels to see how Jesus introduced His parables. They frequently follow some attack by His adversaries and are part of His answer. The topic or general problem is raised first, then the case to be discussed. An illuminating case is found in Matthew 21:33-41, where our Lord, in a moment of controversy, tells the parable of the wicked husbandmen. An owner leases a fertile farm to a group of tenants and at harvest time sends his agents to collect his share. The agents are beaten or killed. Then the owner sends his son, who is also murdered. Then Jesus turns the story over to His hearers. He asks: "When the owner of the vineyard comes, what will he do to those tenants?"

In this case, the response of the crowd has been preserved (like the notes of some modern class observer); they say hotly: "He will put those wretches to death and lease the vineyard to other tenants!" Note that if our Lord had Himself given a similar ending to His story, it would not have been as effective. By leaving the story at the point of decision, He compelled the crowd to become involved and to speak out publicly.

We can do this in our own way and to serve our teaching situation. The point involved is that we want our pupils to practice the application of their Christian standards. Real life calls for swift decisions, and we can help to prepare our children to make them by some practice decisions under guidance. Not alone, but with his classmates and under the teacher, the child deals with sample problems.

This is really a formula device: You start by deciding on an area or topic where you feel the class must face an issue and solve it by Christian standards. The story is built up to lead to the moment when the principal character must do, or not do, something. Right there the story ends, and the class is asked to decide what he will do and why. This is not merely a vote, but generally becomes a lengthy discussion bringing out many shades of opinion. The story may reveal conflicting ideals and even cause heated argument. In due time such earnest talk leads to a search for some authority to say just what really is the Christian thing to do. This is not learned through a neat moral statement from the teacher (who may be somewhat hazy himself about the correct decision), but in the warm exchange of persons.

The following story, in outline form, will illustrate: Boy,

fifth grade, needs fifty cents to complete paying for a football helmet which he feels he needs and has his heart set upon. He had told the other boys he would have it on Saturday. There seems to be no way to get the money. Leaving his schoolroom, he sees a half-dollar on the floor behind the teacher's desk. He puts it in his pocket, starts walking home. Here the story is turned over to the class, with the questions: What did he do? What should he do?

In designing or selecting stories for this purpose, the following points should be observed: (1) Have the principal character the same age as the children in the class, and give him a likely name. (2) Give details of setting and circumstance similar to their own lives or fully familiar to them. (3) Give the principal character some personal desire, attitude, or need that will have a bearing on the incident and his decision at the end. (4) Provide plenty of specific, correct details to give reality. (5) Tell the story well, using all the description and spoken lines that you can invent.

At the end the decision is proposed on two different questions: "What did he do?" asks the children to evaluate the actor's character and temptation as given in the words of the story. The question is worded: "Knowing him as we do, what do you think he did?"

The second question, "What do you think he *should* do?" raises the problem of ideal behavior from each pupil's own point of view. Sometimes this is strict, moralistic, and "right." As often in new situations, the answer is vague or wavering. Through the guided discussion that follows, the Christian ideal involved is clarified. But also it is revealed that decisions are colored by many personal relations and needs and that we are all likely to make wrong decisions when the temptation is too great. Thus the meaning of sin, and later of repentance and redemption, is brought out.

Many of these stories, selected to fit the need to develop certain teaching themes, are now given in the newer textbooks. Others will be shared as they are discovered by earnest teachers. Yet it is possible to invent them for your own use, provided the formula above is fully employed.

Teachers who are genuinely interested in the inner life of their pupils will not only invent these stories, but will discover everywhere anecdotes from real life (true stories) which can be adapted. These are often found in the daily press, and once you begin to recognize them, it is possible to save them for future use.

One last pointer: Keep out of the decision as long as possible. You may rephrase the question and probe for motives, but your own bald statement tends to end discussion. Keep it going! Truth will emerge. By the vital talk of persons who are immersed in real living, partial knowledge is shared, and the result is true learning. And the children love it. One class, after hearing a number of open-end stories, asked the teacher please to finish a story for them. She did, but thereafter they asked: "Oh, let *us decide* after this. We like it better."

15

Start with Life

THE FOLLOWING experiment was tried in a city church for an All Saints' Day session.

Instead of an anecdote about a character of long ago, a story was written by a member of the staff giving a real situation in Manhattan life. A family was described living in the crowded conditions of an apartment. This story was left unfinished, and the pupils discussed what the characters might have said and done. The great interest shown, and the lively prolonged discussion encouraged six other groups to use it. Clearly the secret was that we had put a finger on a sore spot in their own lives and caused them to face it with what Christian helps they could summon. We wanted to teach that sainthood is always won under present pressures and opportunities.

This illustrates what the new way of teaching is proving abundantly: that when we start with life, we get immediate and vigorous response; further, that when a truly real problem is shared by a group, solutions are sought and Christian answers are eventually found.

This is no pedagogic fad, but a rediscovery that comes closer to the ways of our Lord than most people realize. He did not *start* with Scripture (the Old Testament, which He knew). He started with the experience of living people—the people all around Him. From these familiar experiences He turned to the Scripture for illumination: first the experience, then the Scripture. (One exception to this might seem to be in Nazareth, where He read the passage from Isaiah, but this is no exception, because His presence there *was the situation,* which He explicitly claimed in the words: "This day is this scripture fulfilled in your ears." He may have selected the passage Himself.)

In the Gospels we see Jesus speaking to real people, noting their simple, natural outdoor life and the commonplace activities of their day. He moved among people, concerned with their interests and problems, commenting on them with insight and sympathy. He gave *meaning* to what people were doing. If He told a story, it was because it fitted the situation He was describing; it was not merely to entertain. The trouble with many of our teachers is that they know very little of the real lives their children are living.

Yet we may still start with an ideal which we would like to lodge in them. This start takes place, so to speak, behind the scenes and is not evident in the teaching procedure. If you wish to impress, say, the deep satisfaction that follows sacrifice, you do not start with a preachment, nor even with the Bible words, "It is more blessed to give them to receive." This is your secret which you are to hold back until the learners are really seeking it. Rather, you *start* with some reference to life, the real life of your children, and present to their imagination a story that is at first *interesting* (because recognized and familiar in its setting and problems) and then *stimulating* to their imagination and feelings.

This is the art of the designed anecdote, or open-end story, described in the preceding chapter. You can do it. True, a well-designed story already written and tried out by an expert teacher is a great help and can be used by the unskilled teacher, provided he understands the method. But at the present moment not many of these have appeared in print.

Perhaps a collection of useful stories, both fictional and real, will soon be published by some ingenious teacher. In the meanwhile, most of us will have to invent stories or find our own.

Just for the practice, readers might outline the plots of stories designed to start vital discussion leading *toward* the ideal or virtue given. Try some of these: courtesy, forgiveness, family discipline problem, destruction of property, sportsmanship (honest effort) a good loser, showing off versus secret worth or accomplishment, courage, choice, craftsmanship (accuracy, sincerity), or loneliness (friendliness).

Or, decide what is the real goal of your next Sunday's lesson, and cast it into the form of a story from life. After you have done this a few times you will get the feel of it, and you are not likely to go back to the old ways of expounding ancient wisdom.

We used to tell teachers: "Work for response!" But we were clumsy in our devices to this end. The story from life seems to be one solution.

16

Opening a Class Session

"How do you start a class session?" is a question that is being increasingly asked by teachers. The new type of lesson calls for a great deal of pupil response and participation, and teachers are discovering that the flying start may mean the difference between the morning's success or an early relapse into confusion and misbehavior.

"If I can get off on a vital point from the first moment, before they begin to chatter or talk silly, the period will generally go well. If I could only have a good opener always!"

Now it happens that there are plenty of these vital opening moments—call them stunts, devices, approaches, what you will. Every textbook records some, but there is no uniformity in their publication, and many a teacher who could profit by having such an opener all ready to use does not recognize it. Often an activity device suggested for use *later* in a session can well serve as the opening attention-claimer.

Here are a number of tested openers. Do not try to copy these exactly, but make them your own, fitting them to your circumstances and the needs of your children. Once you begin to see the idea, you will be able to decide on a striking one for every Sunday, and you will soon invent plenty of them. Just realize the need that is the mother for this inventiveness: to catch the interest of the class from the first moment in a way that will start conversation along the desired direction leading into a vital discussion.

(1) Ask a provocative question, which will startle the group into attention. You must think this out carefully as part of your advance preparation, and spring it with good timing and dramatic sense. "What would you do if your best friend were killed in an accident?" "How would you feel if someone bombed your school?" "Suppose that you found our church on fire. If you were near, what would you rush in to save?" "Do you wonder why Jesus was born among the Jews and not among us Americans?"

(2) Mention some idea from last Sunday: "We were talking about what June said . . ." (Any carry-over from the preceding lesson is a good opener, provided it had caught the class's attention and was left unsettled.)

(3) If some striking local event, such as an accident or crime, is evidently on their minds, start with that, but have the wit to slant it toward one of your aims. This does not mean providing neat moralizing by the teacher, but letting them discover the religious issue.

(4) "We were talking about allowances last week. Now we are going to form a family conference and see how a home might manage this. John, you are the father. Helen, the mother," et cetera. The teacher will have to set the stage a little and outline the problem and its elements (income, expenses, size of family, et cetera). But this will be a lively subject and may carry over as a starter for several weeks. Remember, you are not settling allowances, but applying some Christian ideals.

(5) Pass out small cards or bits of paper. "When I write this word on the board, you are to write quickly all the words (not sentences) that come into your minds about it. Are you ready?" Write such words as *fear, apology, Saturday morning,*

cowardly, run away. Have the children exchange cards and read them aloud.

(6) Same procedure, but ask everyone to write a definition of some word or doctrine. There will be many strange expressions. (Try this again a month later.)

(7) Bring a mystery box and ask them to guess what is in it. Give some clues. It might contain a crucifix, a letter from a missionary, et cetera.

(8) Start with an open-end story, which ends with a call for some discussion and decision. "Now, what do you think he did—or should have done?" These stories are in many of the new texts, and you can easily make up your own. (See the earlier chapter, "The Open-End Story.")

(9) Start with something from the family service just preceding Sunday school—the minister's talk or a Bible reading.

(10) Begin: "I want each of you to tell of some prayer that was answered—in your own experience or someone else's. I'll call on each of you. I'll give you two minutes to think."

(11) Group Bible study is a good starter. You will have to learn how, but briefly it is this: Write the selected passage on the board, such as I Corinthians 11:26-28. Pass out Bibles to all. Form groups of three. Allow about five minutes for silent reading; then have group discussion. "Decide on the most important idea in this passage." Then call for reports from groups.

Any idea or activity started decisively, well thought out, and calculated to involve everybody in some way, is a good opener. Somebody may compile a book entitled *A Thousand Openers That Have Worked.* Perhaps you will have invented a few and can contribute them. Of course, you might open with prayer!

17

Warming-Up

A TEACHER told a group at an institute: "My most baffling problem is how to get my class interested in my plans. I come all prepared and start to tell them what we are going to do, and they don't seem to care at all. What's the use of preparing if you can't get them to do what you propose?"

This is a far more familiar scene than this teacher realized. And it happens, strangely enough, to some of our most eager and faithful teachers. Indeed, that may be the root of the trouble: the enthusiastic temperament which makes ingenious plans, sees the goal of accomplishment, and then runs up against the apathy of the pupils. It is discouraging and, if repeated often, eventually chills the teacher's ardor, reducing her to a commonplace, routine leader. How to transfer the enthusiasm and purpose of the teacher to the class is the problem.

It is largely a matter of approach and timing. The enthusiastic person expects everybody else to be as keen on his subject as he is, and is a little hurt and rebuffed when he finds people polite but evasive. If you are this type, you should consider how you got that way. Your present hobby, scheme, or project started days ago. Perhaps the main line of it goes back years ago when, by some accidental meeting or reading, you found a certain line of thought captivating your mind. It has been developing slowly in your thinking. Recently it received fresh stimulus and now gushes up, full-tide, in your present enthusiasm. When you speak of it to others, you forget that they have not had the same long, gradual approach.

It is a matter of warming-up. People give themselves to new plans slowly. Here is a committee apathetic to a proposal at the start of the meeting. But by the enthusiasm and skillful presentation of one or two persons, they finally work out a large plan and start on it with eagerness. They have made it their own, but it took an hour or more of talk to reach the point of action.

You find this illustrated in life at every hand. Mother has been working in the kitchen. As she works, her thoughts race on, and she begins to feel she is imposed upon, that somebody else should do some of the housework. She enters the living room, finds the older daughter asleep on the couch. In righteous indignation she insists that Daughter "do her share" and get out the vacuum cleaner at once. Of course, Daughter is annoyed, resists, and there is tension. If she responds, it is under protest, slowly, and with poor spirit. This is almost a parable of the way some teachers launch a project.

What is the better way—the educational way—of getting people into motion? You must realize that you cannot get anybody, any person, warmed up suddenly. People may obey your prodding, but the results are not pleasant.

Therefore, in teaching, map out your approach. Take a long time planning your opening words and anticipating possible reactions to them. Think of ways of referring to the proposal without actually saying: "I want you to do this." Tell of its being done elsewhere, get the class to talking about the problem involved, and ask them for a solution. (That always starts active minds going on their own.) Don't tell them. Hint, play around with the idea. Do you want them to write a letter to a missionary? Then your notes say:

"Fun of getting letters. Cost of postage to foreign lands. How to find out about a Sunday school in Brazil. What if we lived in a far-off land? Can you be a friend with someone you have never seen?" Each of these, in class, will be the push for a separate little sortie into the interests of your pupils.

Give the kettle time. If all goes well and you are a patient and skillful teacher, you will eventually reach the boiling point when somebody says: "Couldn't we . . . ?" and another: "Let's . . ." and a third proposes: "I move we appoint a committee." Then the preliminaries are over. They have made your will their will. They may improve on your plan. They will take all the credit. But it will be your victory.

18

Discussion Is Guided Conversation

WE WERE sitting around the parish house waiting for someone and talking—two teachers and I. The thought ran to our work with children, their interests, some things we had found to work, cases of special response, and our opinions. The one new teacher finally asked me: "What do you think about it? You have been asking us a lot, but you haven't said what you think."

I hesitated because I had decided that, with just these two, here was an opportunity for developing a profitable conversation which would be impossible in the more formal discussion of a larger group. I had really been drawing them out, getting them to begin to say things they needed to say. Naturally I had said little about what I thought.

People have gone zany today over the magic word "discussion." "After the lecture we will have discussion," says the program chairman. Or, the outline says: "Have discussion on this." You would think that any group of people would start to talk up naturally and profitably immediately when "time for discussion" was announced.

It is true that groups must talk and that the influence of the lecturer is diminishing. But the experience of being in a group has a different effect on different people. This is especially true if it is a typical formal meeting with president and secretary at the head table, and the chairs in straight rows. Some will be "hopping up all the time," while others, with even more valuable ideas, will remain silent. The leader does not know the art of getting the quiet ones to speak up, nor of welding individuals into a group mind and purpose. It is an art that can be learned.

With children, discussion is a prime form of self-expression, absolutely necessary to complete the teaching cycle. Yet many teachers do not know how to get it started. Today we realize that discussion is simply guided conversation, often of a highly developed kind. The class is a formal group, but it has the advantage of meeting frequently and of having friendships and relations established and a leader who is trusted.*

The skilled conversationalist, whether with adults or children, tries to draw out the persons with whom he is talking. Some vivacious and eager people can talk readily and often charmingly. But they are not good conversationalists unless they can get the others to talk also. The ready talker (particularly if he has a large store of information and many interests of his own) may easily degenerate into the bore; he never gives you a chance to say what you think. Perhaps he doesn't care. Perhaps, also, he just doesn't know how to ask the right questions to get you started.

In provoking conversation with children, a few points can easily be mastered. First, remember that it is at the level of *opinion* and *familiar experience* that we touch the minds of others. On most common topics everybody has formed some ideas and will express them if given an opportunity. Presented before the group, these are tested and evaluated. Truth is not decided by voting, but intelligent conversation clarifies ideas. The ideas of others are heard, and your own are modified or confirmed. Follow up each answer with that most heart-searching of all questions: "Why do you think

* See also "Lecture or Discuss?"

so?" *But do not argue with the answers given.* This only throws the speaker on the defensive and may set his wrong notion. The group process is more apt to relax him and eventually cause a change.

Second, ask for reactions to the situations presented in the lesson. This is still on the plane of opinion, but it forces the individual to face an idea and phrase it in his own way. "What do you think he should have done?" "Helen, if you had been there, what would you have done?"

Third, "throw it across the table." That means simply to get your pupils to discuss with each other. "John, how would you answer Jane's question?" "How many of you disagree with Tommy? Give him your reasons."

19

The Thinking Time

THE THINKING time always starts with the proposal of some theme that is important and timely to the children. How to launch this period or theme is the first problem of the teacher. The teacher does not announce: "This morning we are going to discuss thankfulness." Rather, she has carefully thought out a representative question designed to create immediate interest and response. It may call for a simple and even obvious answer. These early questions may well be structured to call for a "Yes" or "No" answer. These are sure of getting a response if they deal with a matter of opinion, and not merely with factual information. Later questions will strike deeper, but the openers aim mainly at getting individuals to talk, with their own ideas. Thus: "Are your pets thankful for being fed?"

Some sample openers: "Do you have a place to put your own things at home?" "Do you save your old toys—the ones you used to play with when you were younger?" (The theme will be private property, possessions, and, finally, stealing and respect for the property of others.)

Or the (unannounced) theme is to be courage. "Are you afraid of the dark?" "Do you cry when you cut your finger?" Opening questions should not deal with general knowledge, but should be personal, aimed to touch the private experiences and/or feelings of the child.

A poor opener: "Who can tell me the story of the first Thanksgiving Day?" (This is bad on two counts: it deals solely with factual matter outside the experience of the pupils, and it is thrown out for general response, when, in point of fact, the "brightest" child will likely rush in with a superficial or even an incorrect reply.)

A better opener: "When you have done somebody a favor, do you expect to get paid for it?" Teacher looks around the class, but before the chronic volunteer can answer, she speaks to one—"John?"—and gives John time for a reply, often following up with enough urging to bring out a case that John remembers. Quite as often the question is directed immediately at an individual by name. "George, do you have any special treasures?" The same question may then be asked of several children to get a variety of offerings. All are interested, and shortly the ball is rolling toward thoughts on their feelings about personal belongings.

Once talk is moving, there comes the real probing which gives the name to the "thinking time." You and your pupils together are to get beneath the surface of things to their inner meanings. The first clue to an interpretation of anything is one's own opinion or reaction. The key to this is the phrase: "Why do you think so?" This may prove the most stimulating of all challenges to anyone, young or old.

Thus pressed, anyone may at first reply: "Because it's so! Because I do. Because I always have thought so." Presently one may try to justify his position—that is, rationalize his emotional response to the question. If driven by attack, he may build up a large defense. But if the questioning is gentle and skillful, it may raise the real source of this belief. It may lead to an admission of family origins and early experiences —not today, but in time.

The teacher may turn to others and bring out opinions

that differ. (She does not try to settle the point, but simply to start searching thought.) Here is part of the art of the thinking time: Individuals are helped to express themselves sincerely and directly and in the presence of their friends. Their ideas together or in contrast form the real experience of thinking through a subject.

The talk continues, the teacher drawing out every child on the meaning of the topic. "Do children's opinions matter?" asks an old-timer. Yes, to themselves and to their future. Unless we touch their real life, get it moving along intelligent and purposeful channels, how can we educate?

Such conversation is not the end of the process, but it is a necessary beginning. The tested knowledge of authority (our adult resources) will be brought to bear when needed. But youngsters can be started thinking seriously. And if they do not start early, they may never grow in wisdom. Such guided thought makes the old style of moralizing seem very inadequate.

20

Knowing Your Pupils

"THAT TEACHER had my little girl in her class all year," said a mother, "but at the June picnic she could not call her by name." Thus was this teacher's remoteness from her pupils revealed. She had been dutiful and thorough in the conduct of each class. But she treated the children impersonally as a group, not as real people.

This demand surely comes first and most obviously: to know our pupils, to know them by their correct names just as soon as possible. Many teachers like to put name cards on each child for several weeks—large ones, easily read across the room. In some primary grades the child's name has been painted on his chair. This not only helps his attendance by creating a personal sense of place in the school; it also compels the teacher to know each name. If a new teacher will remember always to address each child by name, he will soon know them. Try having each child sit in the same chair in the circle every Sunday. This causes any absences to stand out, gives each child a feeling of importance, and makes it easy to remember names.

Said a little girl, two weeks after school had started: "My teacher knows my name already. And she always smiles at me." A little thing? No. A vast skill and love was thus revealed, which could open the door to a child's heart.

If you know your children—as persons and also as normal samples of their age group—all teaching is easier. It will change everything you do. First, there is the way of imaginative recall. Remember your own childhood. If you have a class of eighth-graders, you can try to recall what you were like in the eighth grade. Start your imagination running back. Make it a theme for meditation. Think of your own school, its sights and movements. It will begin to come back. You may even jot down a few notes: the look of your home room, the halls, some project in handcraft, some punishment, the games on the playground. (You will not be likely to remember any of the subjects, but rather activities—motion, people, and your share in it all. Let that be a tip to you in planning your own classwork.)

But, second, you will need help in understanding what a child of this age does in school. That calls for the way of visiting. Go to a near-by public school and visit the rooms of the children of the age you teach. You may see some of your own pupils there, and they will be delighted. But you will also see some children at work who are just like those in your class. You marvel that they are so quiet and orderly, when you found your class so boisterous. You begin to take heart. You can do it, too, on Sunday. Then you take a few notes—how they pass the materials, how the teacher speaks softly, how they are required to study their books silently at times. You realize that the room has a character, a definite pattern which is recognized and enforced. The school knows what it wants, and insists on it.

You are now beginning to understand your pupils. Now you must dig beneath the surface, find out what the experts have noted. The third way is some study of child psychology. It is a large subject. But you can start by reading carefully the introduction to your textbook. There may be a bibliography there, too. Your rector can lend you a book. Read particularly the chapters dealing with children of the age you are teaching. You will realize that you knew much of their psychology already, but had not been making use of it. Or, you find that you had been dimly thinking of them with characteristics several years younger (or maybe older) than they are. You will "hit the nail on the head" better after this.

Fourth, you will try to discover their real interests. You should list the familiar experiences of their world and their age, and your list will grow steadily. All your children watch about the same television programs. Start with that.

Children are not concerned with politics or economics. They live mainly in the child's world of home and school. The Seabury Series leads in this quest for children's real interests and concerns. Your concern as a teacher is to discover the different, special interests of each child. One approach has been to ask the parents, by means of a letter, to tell you some of the special hobbies and activities of their child. Most parents will gladly answer such questions as these: His favorite television programs? How often does he watch? Activities —sports, games? Does he do any reading? Companionship with any adults? Neighborhood playmates? Say his prayers?

For all this material, a confidential section in your notebook will help you as the year advances. There will be a page or space for each child, and this will gradually fill with brief memos. Here also you will note, after some class periods, revealing words and actions of each child.

Finally, and all through, there is the way of friendship. You will come to share the life of each child, and they will love and follow you in whatever you suggest.

21

Too Much Storytelling

IF YOU ask the average middle-aged person to explain what he considers the work of the Sunday school teacher, he will very likely define it as "to teach the children all the Bible stories." Or he may say: "Telling the Bible story, and then showing its application—pointing the moral." This concept prevails among people whose background is that of nineteenth-century Protestantism, and especially among those who once had a class in an old-fashioned "Bible school."

When we tell such people that we now have other methods and that the telling of Bible stories is not the main goal in our schools today, they are shocked and reply with indignation: "That's just the trouble. You don't teach the Bible any more."

The foregoing reveals how thoroughly we have become involved in a program of teaching which is prepared to deal only with immature minds. Storytelling is a teaching device to hold the interest of the simple and childlike mind. The stories, however, should be preliminary to the imparting of other truths—they are form and container, not content. In a strictly children's program, the storytelling method might well be the main method or approach. Until recently we have seldom taught successfully persons above about fourteen years of age. Yet it is the real Bible, the genuine inner substance of the Bible teaching, which it is our duty to impart. Not more than one-third of the Bible is narrative; the rest is poetry, theology, and Christian experience.

Today all too many of our teachers undoubtedly still look upon telling-the-story as their prime duty. Let's see how we got this way. It first arose, as mentioned, from the concept of a children's program. Then came the crystallization of this Bible-story approach in several series of published textbooks and lesson systems. Its backbone has probably been the International Lesson series with its schedule of Bible passages. If you assume this Bible-story approach, it is easy to get the impression that the Bible is simply a sequence of stories. Starting with the Old Testament, you discover that from the first pages, book after book, the material is largely narrative. This lasts through the first seventeen books—that is, through Esther. Job has even been presented as a story, though it is scarcely edifying for juniors. So the storytellers have to skip all the prophets, pausing only for a few stories from Daniel.

The stories begin again with the opening page of the New Testament, and once more there is action (narrative) through five books. This situation ends abruptly with the Book of Acts. From Romans through Revelation there are no stories (except events that can be deduced) , and therefore the story-telling system misses this richest area of the Bible. It is in these portions of *interpretation* of the historic Biblical action —in the prophets and the epistles—that we find much of the treasures of Bible truth. Unless we teach these, we are not teaching the Bible.

Some teachers do little more than tell stories; then they hope to "bring out the meaning." But they call for no drill, no handwork, no guided discussion, no memorizing, no homework, no study. The story does not spring from the child's real interest, nor with any clear teaching goal. Moreover, many Bible stories have doubtful "morals" for certain ages. The storytelling approach as the one and only way, is probably giving us much weak and inadequate teaching. It may account for many bored or boisterous classes.

For the stories are seldom well told and, indeed, are seldom even *told! I suspect that three-fourths of the stories presented before classes on a given Sunday morning are read aloud from a book or leaflet.* In most cases the reading is from "cold copy"—that is, without any advance preparation. And the children have heard most of the stories before.

But, you ask, isn't storytelling one of the great arts of teaching? It is indeed. But not *that* way, not with that approach.

22

The Right Use of Stories

IF THEN—as we said above—you are not to *read* the story to the class, how will you present it? The answer is that stories are a form of dramatic representation and, as such, call for a living actor or speaker. It is true that they come to us in printed form, and the poor storyteller argues that they are told so much better by the author that they might as well be read to the children exactly as written. This would seem to be true in some cases, with unusually vivid writing.

But teachers who have learned how to tell stories in their own words—looking into the eyes of their eager listeners, without notes, and free to make gestures—will not go back to reading aloud. It is true that the teller's words and style may not be quite as polished as the more literary story, but he has made it his own, and it gets across as no reading ever does. Moreover, it must often be true that a teacher reads from the book because he will not take the trouble to prepare himself to tell the story. This is a constant temptation, and it is often hard to convince a teacher that he is covering up his real motive, which is to do it the easier way.

Success and long experience in telling stories, after proper preparation, give a satisfaction and confidence that proves the value of the trouble involved. Once you know the power and pleasure of holding the attention of a group, you will not cheapen your performance by reading aloud.

Ages of mankind's experience produced the story. It was the simplest means of reporting an experience to the young; it was the codified memory of the tribe. The storyteller not only entertained, but instructed and admonished. Primitive people, like children, could understand the story and admired the storyteller. The long line of scalds, jongleurs, and bards of Europe were storytellers.

Jesus, with other teachers of His day, used the story. The thirty distinct parables of our Lord which have survived in the Christian Scriptures are unquestionably the most beautiful and forceful teaching stories known to mankind. Why did He use the parable? Says Trench: "Had our Lord spoken naked spiritual truth, how many of His words—partly from His hearers' lack of interest in them, partly from their lack of insight—would have passed away from their hearts and memories, leaving scarcely a trace behind?" Indeed, is not this the sacramental principle, derived from the Incarnation: that the outward form conveys the inward and spiritual truth which would otherwise be too elusive to be appreciated?

The story, then, is an age-tested device for teaching. It was and is still the first and most elementary method. But it must not be considered the only method. To the teacher who will take storytelling seriously and will work for skill in it, there are open doors ahead. The following are a few suggestions:

Don't use up your story in the opening moments of your class. It is too precious to waste. Because of its attention-getting quality, you will need it later in the class period. Build up *toward* your story by discussion, by directed conversation, or by other devices.

Decide first the theme which you wish to illustrate; then select a story to accomplish this. It is true that often the editor has made this decision for you by selecting both the theme and the story. You may accept his choice, or you may wish to make your own selections. In any event let's not tell a story just because it is in the Bible.

Put all speeches into quotes. This means that you think out, in your preparation, lines for each character to say. Weak: "He told his father that he had been bad." Strong: "The prodigal said, 'Father, I have sinned. . . .' "

Make characterization vivid. You may have to provide descriptions, actions, gestures. But make your listeners *see* the people you are presenting in your tale.

Use rhythmic repetition, using a catch phrase or term over and over throughout the story like the refrain of a song. The children love it, and it helps them remember and retell the story.

23

Difficult Children

WHAT CAN we do about the child who disrupts the class by bad conduct, yields to no ways of discipline that we have tried, and is the despair of the teacher? Here are some typical cases:

Case 1. Boy, 7, in second grade. Can't keep his hands from other children. Is always pinching, poking, or twisting an arm. Teacher tries to have him sit next to her, but he still bothers the nearest child. No amount of scolding or even minor punishment can make him long desist. He is not subnormal, but seems to have a wrong attitude toward other children. It has been noticed that he likes to draw freehand for short periods. Otherwise, he refuses to do what the rest of the class is doing, will not obey simple requests. He comes alone; parents do not attend church. But he never misses, likes to be there.

Case 2. Boy, 8, in third grade. Extra bright and keen. Talks in loud voice, interrupts teacher and other pupils. Has an opinion, expressed freely, about everything. At times the teacher seems to have won his coöperation; then he becomes difficult again. The teacher is very patient, really likes the boy. An only child, his father died two years ago. Can't seem

75

to interest him in ordinary class procedures, nor to divert his excessive talking.

Case 3. Boy, 13, in seventh grade. Grandmother brought him in middle of year. She explained that he had caused trouble in two other Sunday schools, but hoped this church could "do something with him." He is overweight, strong, and the other children seem a little afraid of him, although he does not show signs of being a bully. Rather low I.Q., does not catch ideas quickly. The problem is his destructiveness. He breaks pencil points deliberately, tears books, cuts up paper with scissors, leans back on chair legs and has broken two chairs. Yet a very likable boy, always cheerful and agreeable. Teacher is a meticulous, careful person who had the class in perfect order until he came. She has asked the superintendent to transfer him to another class.

Analyze these cases, and say what you would do for each. These and many other cases remind us that teaching in the church school is not easy and that often one such child can take all the pleasure out of it. One solution proposed for the last case is to try the child in another class; but this is not solving the problem for the child. In a few extreme cases of unmanageable conduct which we have known, the firm help of parents has been called for. Can we ever expel a child? At what point of failure to fit our school can we ask parents to take back their child and try other ways? Granted that many of our church teachers are amateurs and that we should not expect too much of them, how can we reinforce their control?

On one side, difficult children are the teacher's personal challenge. He may long for tractable, self-controlled children, who do just as he wishes. Sometimes you get a whole class like this, and the year's work is a dream of order and easy teaching. We must deal with the few who are not so calm, and solve their problem if we can.

The overactive, noisy, obstreperous child may only be demanding more purposeful *activity*, less talk, in the class. He may be a barometer of the teacher's inadequate planning, of failure to evaluate correctly the true needs of the class. There should be created a vital and continuing *purpose* in the class. "We are making this. We need these materials. We will show our work at the parent-teachers meeting."

Let the class have fun, but quickly break up all silliness and crazy giggling. Teachers get about the kind of conduct they expect. Few really *want* confusion, but they have become resigned; they cease to struggle. Gradually and without the teacher's realizing it, a class may take on a character of boisterousness, disrespect, and laxity, which may prove hard to break up. Often, if this is the case, it may require several Sundays given over to vigorous corrective methods to end this and to start a new tone.

Unquestionably the newer courses, in which a theme (with an activity accompanying it), is carried over several Sundays, help to create better discipline and class morale. There are several reasons for this. The class becomes a group, united for a purpose, and carries along the odd ones in its tide of interest. Starting from some vital interest in their own lives (not starting from a moral maxim or even a Bible passage), all members find that they want to say something. The ones who seemed to resist the common life before, now find they are persons in a community and, in working out their relationship with the others, come to a new sense of their own real importance. They may not know this, indeed, but the teacher or some wise observer can detect their growth. The teacher himself becomes a member of the fellowship and is accepted as an intimate rather than taskmaster. And the teacher may feel his own personhood enhanced as he takes his place among these eager young friends.

We must provide outlets for the show-off, if possible.

"Johnny has a funny story to tell. We are going to ask him to stand up and tell it." He may suddenly retire at the idea, or if he performs, *that* is over and done with.

Hands must do something. Be swift and firm in ending any physical interference by one child with another—pinching, shoving, hitting, kicking under the table, grabbing another's books. "We just don't stand for that!" Then provide something physical to do.

Set up your class in physical comfort from the start: all outer coats and overshoes removed and out of the way, little girls' gloves and purses put aside. Allow nothing in hands until the moment for using it, and keep things out of sight until then. This means pencils, paper, crayons, paste, scissors, and even Bibles and other books.

Always be in the classroom first; catch every eye as the children enter; start with a vital thought or action well prepared. Don't call the roll at the start. Don't start with a review of last Sunday's lesson—unless it is a going activity or concern, and then be prepared to carry it on farther.

There is a limit, no doubt, to what can be expected of the teacher. The parish administration, represented immediately in the person of the superintendent, must be alert to step in and help. A teacher should feel able to send a disruptive child to the "office," as in any well-managed school. Whole schools take on a better tone once it is realized that the organized parish is behind the school and that much is expected of every person.

Difficult children are not only the naughty ones, who make it hard to teach; they are frequently the quiet and obedient ones who cause us no trouble, but whom we know we are not reaching. In this sense every pupil is difficult, each one a problem to be solved.

24

Questioning for Concerns

"I HAD an interesting experience recently," a teacher reported. "We had finished our Bible lesson, and the talk seemed to turn about their parents. I asked, 'Do you ever get angry with your father or mother?' At once they had plenty to talk about."

One boy told how his mother often made him mad. The others contributed similar stories. "I didn't scold them," said the teacher. "I just let them talk. Sometimes I asked them a question to draw out their story—whether they stayed mad very long, whether it was the child or the parent who was to blame for the anger, and so on. Then I asked one boy what he did when his mother yelled at him, and how he felt. They all had something to say."

This teacher had stumbled upon an area of education largely ignored, because of our fixed goals, until now. She added, "I wish I could get a conversation like that going again. And I wish I might turn it into a religious discussion."

She can get it going again, and often, if she will turn her attention to exploring the real world of childhood, and she will discover that it will be religious. Not accidentally, but by ways that are known, it is possible to enter into this world.

The way to find out what children are thinking is to ask them. Simple, isn't it? We have guessed, we have written and read learned books on child psychology. We have not thought to ask children, typical and otherwise, what was going on in their minds.

The goal of teaching in the past was causing pupils to digest a lot of information. You got this "knowledge" into them by what charm, hammering, coaxing, or other methods you could manage. Then, as part of the method, you drilled them on it. You asked them questions about it. If they could give it back accurately, you felt they had it, and you knew you were a successful teacher.

This narrow use of the art of questioning produced the reviews, test questions, final written examinations, and factual recall which were, we now realize, the obvious devices required by a content-centered curriculum. This must, no doubt, always be the case where information—"objective facts" some educators called them—is the goal. But what our pupils *think* is not mere "subjective illusion." This is life itself, their real inner life with which we must deal. We may hope to modify it, but first we must touch and understand it.

If you want to find out what a person thinks about anything, ask him. If you really *want* to know what is on a person's mind—his enthusiasms, his dreads and worries, his groping and misunderstandings, the people who trouble him and those whom he trusts—then you are on the way toward the new kind of teaching. The method is basically rather simple. When you have seen it done a few times, you can try it and improve with practice.

The first step is to write down a number of questions and to learn to distinguish between questions asking for *facts* and those asking for *opinions*. A sample of this is found in the stock questions often asked visiting celebrities by reporters. "Are you afraid of communism in your country?" "Would you like to live in America?" "What do you think of American women?" Some of the questions asked are often absurd, but they do reveal the mind of the visitor.

Here are some questions of fact taken from some older textbooks: "Why do Christians keep Sunday instead of the Jewish Sabbath?" "What does the word *creed* mean?" "What voice did Paul hear on the road to Damascus?" "What are the names of the twelve apostles?" "In what sermon will you find the Golden Rule?"

In contrast, here are some questions that might be asked of children to reveal their present experiences and thoughts: "Do you like to go for a walk with your father?" "Do you think you should be punished for tearing your clothes?" "When a big boy is mean to smaller children, how do you feel?" "Does your mother ever get mad at you?" "Do you ever look up at the stars?" "Do you think they will have a man land on the moon?" "What things make you mad?" "Are you afraid in the dark?" "What is your most treasured possession?"

The real difference is not between facts and opinions, but between *general* questions about ancient history, remote from the child's life, and *personal* questions about his doings and feelings and the striking events of his world.

Why should we do this? Because, unless minds meet, there can be no real communication. Our children's minds are occupied with their daily experiences in home, in school, and at play. About all these they have strong feelings—of apprehension, resentment, and frustration, or of satisfaction, delight, security, excitement, and achievement. By touching these you are able to reach and help the real child.

The older approach, being centered in the "lesson material," used questioning simply as a check on whether the children had listened. There was a boy who asked his teacher as a little joke: "Why do teachers ask questions?" and who gave the answer: "Because they don't know themselves." As a matter of fact, by the old way the reverse was more often true: the teacher knew the exact answer—she often had it printed in the book she was holding—and wanted to hear a pupil repeat it. This inadequate performance has passed as "response" or "drill" in the minds of many.

Can an inexperienced teacher learn to ask personal questions? Unquestionably, but it will require practice and some advice. Try writing out some questions in preparation for a lesson. Choose an area in which your class is now involved, and think of forms in which this might occur in the children's lives. In a way you will be aiming, at long range, at your subject. Yet your questions are much more than an opening zone of interest merely to bring up your subject before launching into the "topic for today." You are to think out some possible ways of entering into the children's real experiences and of developing these in leisurely, yet penetrating, dialogue. Don't worry about getting into your subject. They will get into it by any number of unexpected, sudden openings. But it will be their subject then—not one forced on their attention.

The prim teacher hears an incorrect or unorthodox answer and takes time out to beat it down with the correct information. She won't let untruths be uttered in her class! But listen to a skilled teacher who cares about her pupils. She accepts their replies courteously because they are honest and sincere. She will neither praise nor blame—just sympathetic acceptance and a swift passing-on to the next question, or perhaps the deft: "Why do you think so?" There are no star performers; no one is put to shame. The purpose is to secure an honest, original response, shared with the others. Here are some of the topics the children will discuss revealingly: punishment and discipline, the strict parent and teacher (children prefer them), stealing, lying, prayer, God, making things, conscience, anger, death, worry, racial prejudice, secrets, friends, good losers, sharing.

This method is not a new system, not an end. But it is a new beginning. Until we know what is on the minds and in the feelings of our pupils, what we offer makes very little contact.

A pioneer in this work is Helen Parkhurst, whose book, *Exploring the Child's World* (New York: Appleton-Century-Crofts, 1951), describes her many conversations with real children and is recommended to all who wish to learn the child's point of view.

25

The Class Observer

THE TEACHER who is eager to get results and who often feels dreadfully alone, in need of guidance, will welcome the plan of having a working assistant. This function is now well established and is beyond the stage of experiment. It is a known and tested way of improving teaching. Moreover, with our emphasis on touching the actual lives of the pupils, it is vastly important that we understand and control what is really happening in each class period.

This second adult leader in each class is not established as a kind of spy or reporter to the parish of the correctness of the teacher's performance. He or she becomes with practice a working partner. He is not another teacher—although he is ready, in emergencies, to take over the teaching—but his function is to watch, listen, and take notes. Later he will confer with the teacher, and together they will evaluate and plan for coming lessons. The two together form a true teaching team. There are two adult minds and judgments working on the week-by-week problem, where before the teacher worked alone.

Once enlisted, this extra person has an increasingly vital share in the strategy of the year's work. The duties undertaken will depend partly on the training, outlook, and capabilities of the observer, but these duties will broaden with practice.

At first the observer may be simply an assistant, doing the small things that take the teacher's time and releasing her to concentrate on the direct management of the group. These things include recording the roll, preparation and handling of supplies, children's coats, hats, purses, gloves, and all such matter of movement. He will handle any points of discipline and class disturbance. He will be free to deal with individual children if need be. All the while he will be watching an experienced teacher at work and thus preparing to be a teacher some day perhaps himself. This level of help may go on for some weeks, as the observer becomes adjusted to the class situation and gets acquainted with the children. If incapable of doing anything further, he will certainly be of great help just in these things. Beginners may stay at this stage or advance to the next, as they discover the possibilities.

The deeper level of observing, for which the office has been primarily created, is an extremely sensitive and expert entering into the movements of the class. He is to catch, so far as his judgment and training enable him, the actual relationships that are developing between the teacher and the group of pupils as they respond to each other through the year. The observer notes what is really happening in the class.

He will quite naturally become informed of the subject matter and plan of the year's work. But this is not his assignment. He is to note the *process;* that is to say, he will try to detect the personal reactions and the undercurrents revealed by both the conversation and the actions of the class. He will always be alert to clues, in words or actions, which might reveal personality. This is interpretation, although without the heavy hand of closed judgment. "Why did he say that?"

"What is the probable significance of this child's changed attitude toward another or toward the teacher?"

The children soon accept the observer as part of their class experience. If told that he is writing down some of the things they say, they may ask: "What did I say today?" But this is only for a while, and they soon are accustomed to this other adult friend who usually sits quietly watching and taking notes. Some observers enter into the teaching at times, supplementing the words of the teacher. But if they do this too frequently, the desired effect of the personal leadership of the one teacher is dissipated.

How is an observer enlisted? Any intelligent and spiritually minded person will do, even without experience, but he or she should be mature in age and outlook. He should surely have a definite religion of his own. Some knowledge of educational theory and child psychology would be helpful, though not requisite. Many teachers, desiring a helper, have enlisted a personal friend. The working together as a class team increases their companionship and sympathy. The two can readily get together and discuss progress each week. Husband and wife form a splendid teaching pair—possible where one does not have to stay at home with tiny children.

Usually the parish leader has to find and assign a new observer. When it is generally known that a whole new set of helpers is wanted in the school, enlistment becomes easier. It is now generally recognized to be unwise to advertise by general notice or appeal in the parish bulletin that "we desire volunteers for teachers." This is so because nobody replies, or persons unsuited in age, training, or temperament may respond. *Teachers* should be carefully picked, prepared, and placed. *The observer,* on the other hand, while an important functionary, can well be a volunteer enlisted by a general appeal, or any available person who seems to have possibilities.

One of the advantages of this new post for parish leadership strategy is that the observer is himself being trained and watched and may be shifted about. Thus, a person tries himself and is tried out for real interest in children. Many people warm to teaching gradually, and by this approach a steady supply of new teachers is made available. Indeed, the observer is actually in training by being immersed in the very process. Thus, many parishes find observers by asking people who seem potential teachers, but who lack confidence and experience. Their work as an observer plunges them immediately into the full tide of teaching, without danger of making mistakes. It would seem from past efforts in the Church that this may at long last prove to be the best way to carry on a continuous program of teacher-training. Under thorough supervision observers are themselves watched, their efforts are guided, and they may be assigned different classes through the year for their own experience. It is good for the teachers, too, to have a change of observer. Often we find that the newly assigned observer takes over the function of the teacher, and the two reverse roles, by mutual agreement. A breakdown of the plan was reported in the case of the teaching team who decided that it was needless for both to be present every Sunday, and so arranged to serve on alternate Sundays!

The observer is expected to be present *every* Sunday and to confer with the teacher at some time between sessions. Inevitably, in the many pressures of family life today, there must be absences, but the teaching team makes it nearly always possible to have at least one person present. The teacher can work alone, or the observer, knowing the pupils and the course, can carry on without a break, and no outside substitute teacher is needed. This gives great flexibility to the teaching staff, and continuity of teaching.

The appeal by the leader when enlisting workers is twofold: To persons invited to be observers he can say: "We can use you in our new system. I realize you have no experience and cannot imagine yourself as a teacher. But as an observer you will be able to see if this appeals to you, and at the same time you will be receiving training on the job under a skilled teacher. You may like the work and grow. If not, you can drop out without hurting the school."

To persons known to have the ability to teach, but who decline because of the burden, the appeal is: "You will not bear the whole responsibility of the class. You will have companionship and encouragement from an observer."

To any teacher, old or new, this idea is offered urgently. If your parish has not yet moved toward this plan for an assistant in each class, you can find your own observer and try it out. The actual work of observing and of planning together is a highly skilled art, but one that can be learned. The newer textbooks give necessary instructions for its use. One point needs stressing: the conference between teacher and observer is essential if the full benefit of the plan is to be realized. This separate meeting of the two each week may prove difficult. That is why family teams are good, or friends who live close together. We have heard of two women who work in the same office forming a team and conferring at lunch.

One variation that has proven feasible is this: the observer as usual makes notes on the day's page in his notebook and on the individual pages for each child, dating each entry. Then the two linger briefly after class to mention some special points that have arisen, and the teacher takes the observer's notebook home. It will be read at the time of preparing the following Sunday's session, and the notebook is simply handed back to the observer at the start of the new period. Thus, the accumulating notes of the course are always in the teacher's hand and are a help in charting the movement of the class.

PART III

Group Life

26

Your Class Becomes a Group

WITH ALL the new talk about "group process"—and the increased understanding of the vast possibilities in "group life" —it is well that teachers in our church schools try to become familiar with it. It is not a fad, for it is well past all experimental first stages. Nor is it a panacea—a marvelous new trick which will solve all teaching problems. But it is an area in which we were almost entirely blind for years, yet it is an experience deep in the nature of the Christian community. It may be traced readily in many forms in glimpses of the early Church revealed in the New Testament.

The ordinary Sunday school class may become a group, although this requires time and development. When people are first thrown together for any meeting—social or sports or business—they may be called a *grouping,* but they do not become a *group* in the new technical sense until they have gone through certain stages of growth. They must develop a common life, with a real interplay of persons. Social scientists recognize three stages:

(1) *Dependence.* In this initial stage, when the people of the group first meet, there is the usual formal etiquette— politeness, but reserve. Feelings are hidden. The current clichés are exchanged. The conversation deals with the ob-

vious, and no one feels the urge to communicate. They are in each other's presence, but they are separated, as it were, by a transparent envelope.

(2) *Independence.* This may start fairly early in the life of the grouping. It is a revolt by its several members against the prim dullness of the first stage. People become aware of each other as beings who either threaten their position or may be useful as an audience for their ego. Here is self-expression at its lowest level. Person competes with person for recognition and status. The bore (the naïve enthusiast who needs to tell somebody about himself because he lacks the confidence gained by real achievement and recognition) now corners you. Hostilities arise as insecure persons feel the need to attack or defend. This is the "scrappy" stage reached by many a club, fraternity, auxiliary, or family. It may take some time to pass through it.

(3) *Interdependence.* Here, when sparring is no longer necessary and conflict has been found to have no satisfaction, good impulses begin to come to the light, and people start being truly unselfish, sincere, and interested in the lives of the rest. Problems that exist between individuals or between small cliques are worked out. People feel free to say what they really mean and want, and they try honestly to listen and understand the others, even the most annoying.

Up to this point the development might take place in any grouping moving toward becoming a real group. But if the gathering—of the same persons regularly over a period of time—be of Christians, in the name and under the aims of the Church, something else is discovered. Any human group may develop an *esprit de corps*—whether the Marines, a club, lodge, school, company, or team. This is not recognizable as the Holy Spirit, although we must be ready to admit that He may work through any group. But in a church group, when its life has continued long enough to have developed into the third stage above, the peculiar spirit working through the Holy Community is none other than God, the Holy Spirit. This is what raises this new group dynamics from the area of psychology to that of religion.

Let us be clear: The Holy Spirit is forever seeking us. We are told to wait upon Him. The intelligent and reverent use of group methods may prove a fruitful way of providing a readiness for His inflowing. When the day of Pentecost was come, the disciples were together in one place (the Scripture repeats, at the expense of being redundant). They had continued together day after day—obedient, expectant, with the same hope. We can be sure that they had come to know and trust each other. And so the Spirit came to them.

What has this to do with the ordinary church school class? A great deal. Your class may become a group, an intimate fellowship of understanding, sharing, interdependent persons. Their age does not matter. The teacher must come to appreciate the possibilities of having the same pupils together week after week. You may linger long in the early stages, but now and then you will find times when the third stage has been granted to you.

You may plan and guide a little by ways that can be learned. But the final experience is a gift from above. Your children are no longer your listeners, nor even your "charges." You and they together are living out your lives, by frequent interchanges, in one corner of the Spirit-filled beloved community.

NOTE: Other methods that will help in creating a group are suggested in "The Thinking Time," "Start with Life," and "Questioning for Concerns."

27

Group Dynamics in the Classroom

The central idea of group life is essentially simple: We learn to *live together* by being together—that is to say, by learning the limits within which we can be ourselves in relation with others. We *learn* most readily by thus being together. The Church has always known this in a general way, but we have only recently discovered how to make use of this truth, which was inherent in the early Church. "How these Christians love one another," an enemy observed. They kept coming together, to be with each other, and to be with their Lord who, they believed, was present when they came together in the Sacrament.

We lost this sense of the power latent in group life in the traditional Sunday school of the past hundred years. The teacher was trained to teach each child his lesson: that is, each child learned directly from the teacher the same subject matter. Some learned better than others because some worked harder or were brighter. It was thought that it was a combination of brains and diligent study (plus a strict teacher) which resulted in a brilliant scholar. He went through the prescribed routine, grade by grade, and was graduated into adult life, an educated person.

There have always been collections of children, indeed, grouped by ages into classes. But the class was only an aggregation of individual pupils—an economy because a dozen or more could listen to the teacher as well as one. This inadequate conception of the class still remains in many a church school. All the while teachers have been missing the creative possibilities which were untapped, just below the surface, in the composite life of the individuals seated before them.

All this is available to us through a right understanding of group dynamics. It is not a trick of words; its language is fluid and changing. It is a reality, a way, an ancient truth. Like the heavy metals just now being discovered and put to terrific use, it has been there always. Like uranium, too, we may find that it can be used for both destructive and creative purposes. When Christians meet under right conditions, there is hidden power that may be released. Like atomic power, it was always there, unrealized, generally unused.

What is a group, then, if not just a number of folks? For our purpose, a group should fulfill these requirements: (1) Several people, (2) meeting frequently, (3) the same persons at every meeting, (4) in sympathy with a common goal, (5) which no member can hope to reach alone, (6) gradually affecting one another, (7) reaching decisions and carrying out plans impossible alone, and (8) as a result *learning* more and better than they could by any other means.

Notice how all these points apply to your church school class. Here they are as you join their circle on Sunday (do not confront them from behind a desk). The stage is set, the curtain is rising. What will happen? Will you give them a sage monologue about ancient lore, until they become restless? Or will you give them the opportunity to be a group? Are you going to be authoritarian and dominate the whole period by your thoughts and words? Or are you willing to learn the new way of group life, and let them become a group?

The principal device of group expression is discussion. This we have known and used for some time, but too often in a stiff and thwarting manner. We prefer now to speak of it as "conversation," or "dialogue"—the meeting of minds and the sharing of partial knowledge. But this is to be no shapeless and chatty babbling. The teacher is going to learn how to lead, but not dominate. He will discover how to give the right nudge when needed, and how to bring the talk back to the desired channel when it gets out of hand. Yet he recognizes and utilizes the contributions of the class.

This is the logic of the teaching process that makes use of this untouched group vitality: you cannot hope to impart any of your knowledge (the "lesson" or the "aim for today") until you have brought about a community of interest and an interplay of the active minds of your pupils. You will probe along the line of your planned approach, but what you bring up may be quite different from what you had expected. You can hope to steer, but until there is some common movement, there is nothing to steer.

Children (yes, everyone!) yearn to express themselves. Each wants the esteem of others; each wants the human dignity of being a person among persons. They want the security of belonging; they want, vaguely, to do things that they know they cannot do alone. And they really want guidance, though not the heavy dominance of an adult who does not appreciate their needs.

And you read them a story, and then ask them to crayon a printed outline or fill in the blanks in a workbook!

Your class is a little world, a life within the larger life. Here in a Christian group they are experiencing human relations on a plane they will never encounter elsewhere. The class is not your audience. It is a fellowship of which you are one member. Its vital expression is conversation, and then common tasks, carried through by division of efforts. But it is always "our exhibit" and "we decided."

When a congenial company, of adults or of children, come together, something happens that could never have happened to them alone. They will talk of the things that are closest to their interests. Out of their shared opinions, confidences, reactions, memories, and experiences will be kindled a strange new "light that never was on sea or land." It will not be merely the sum total of the minds of a dozen outspoken, eager people, but a group mind, a corporate entity, which flows from them, yet to which they give themselves as to a river in full flood. They have created it, by God's grace, yet each is still vividly himself within it, while each one feels his share in the larger life. To give yourself and your pupils this rich experience not once, but steadily, is your opportunity as a class teacher. Once you begin to grasp it or stumble upon it in a moment of selfless leading, you will never forget it. You will seek it again and improve your use of it. Then your teaching will have a power you never dreamed of.

28

Let the Children Plan

THE SUCCESSFUL church school class is always either starting or carrying through some interesting activity. Visiting a school in action, one sees one class listening listlessly to the teacher's talk, another class that has broken out into uncontrolled noise. But here is a class busy and purposeful. There is talk back and forth, not only between teacher and pupils, but between pupil and pupil. They are all interested. They seem to be doing something together in which all are involved.

What has led up to this? The answer is that the teacher has learned how to use the art of democratic class-planning. He has discovered that until his class has developed a mind and purpose of its own as a group, it is composed of solitary individuals, though seated side by side. If only he can get them to be a group, to want to do something together! But how?

An inadequate way, abundant experience has shown, is for the teacher to bring a preconceived plan before the class and put it through by any means. Here we must look into the temperament of the teacher and his conception of group life. If he is naturally original, inventive, and ingenious, as well as skilled in varied manual arts, he may often bring to the class wonderful schemes to make, to do. He brings all the patterns, materials, and tools—that is, he used to do this,

98

until he found himself bucking a mysterious dead center of inertia, and he now seldom uses more than the old stick-to-the-book ways.

With the newer ways of class-planning, it should be cautioned, the same aggressive ingenuity may be shown by some pupil who, when suggestions are invited, comes up with a full-blown plan, which he proposes as the activity of the class. This Napoleonic type of child needs special handling or he may emerge in adult life as a hair-trigger imaginer, a brilliant schemer, and in his turn become a dominating—and frustrated—teacher. Such an individual can be guided and his imaginative fountain utilized by the devices of democratic planning. Other children may warm up more slowly, but their ideas, too, are to be welcomed.

It should be made clear that group-planning takes place mainly through discussion. Plans take shape gradually as many minds address themselves to a problem. Two stages, which blend into each other, must be appreciated by the teacher. First, there is the emergence of the problem, when it may be only dimly felt as a problem. *Take time* to let this develop. Once the children see that there is a problem and have identified and accepted it, they are ready to propose a solution.

Second, there is the stage of planning. In more complicated projects this may require several Sundays. Ordinarily this is more like the deliberations of a committee. Having accepted an assignment, they ask: "What can we do?" And then: "How shall we do it?" Here the teacher who is habituated either to brilliant leadership or to old-style solo teaching must get a new view. He must learn to trust his pupils. He must come to believe that there are ideas in their minds often superior to his own. And he should not be surprised if they improve on his suggestions. Most important, he must come to see that when they accept a plan as their own, an educational experience starts. This is not to say that ingenious and novel schemes that the teacher has discovered or invented should not be used. Most often his plan will be the best or only one suitable. The point is that the class must *seem to make it their own.* The class may be shy at first, as though amazed that their teacher really wants them to decide. Then one day this democratic planning clicks quite unexpectedly: a scheme is hatched and carried out.

The teacher may come prepared with certain plans, but he is ready to see them modified or scrapped. He must be prepared to stimulate pupil interest but also, as interest is engendered, to allow the class to have its own way.

Planning is not a single decision, but takes shape as the details emerge. How shall we get there? What materials will we need? Who will bring the books? Who will find out about the place? How much money will we need?

You'll have few problems of discipline once your class learns to plan and carry through. You'll hardly know it as the same class.

Only one caution need be added. Don't count too heavily on the children's coming up with a suitable, novel plan. They may propose schemes too grandiose, requiring much time, expensive materials, and skills beyond them. Or they may suggest only the worn-out projects that have been done for years or ones suited to the public school. Let the teacher have his plans, but be prepared to let them be much modified by the class.

29

The Organized Class

WHEN A class has developed group spirit, all teaching is easier. The very fact of having the same individuals together for an hour every week means that here is a miniature world, a complete society. Living together as Christians is one of our main goals. This means that in the Church—the home parish, among actual, present fellow churchmen—we practice the Kingdom of God.

Here under Christian leadership boys and girls have experiences in thinking, planning, and acting together as Christians practicing their religion in a real world. There is no group like it anywhere else.

How to make children keenly aware of their group and to create this group, or class, consciousness *quickly* is a real problem. The primitive desire is present already in the gang instinct of growing children. But the impulse and drive to forge this class awareness—so that the children think and speak of "our class"—must come from the will and purpose of the teacher. He must always speak and think of "us," never of "my class."

First, the class should be organized. Groups of approximately the ages nine through fourteen are the best. Even older classes may profit from being organized, since parliamentary procedure is part of the democratic method, and its machinery helps to expedite many activities. (Time is wasted in trying to organize younger children; they are not ready for it.)

At the opening meeting in the fall, the talk may be directed to the matter of class spirit—loyalty to each other, et cetera. "We all want to have a strong class, don't we? Would it help if we organize, with officers?" After the desire is created—but not at the opening session—candidates are agreed upon and later elected.

These will include a president and a vice-president and, if the school approves, an attendance secretary. You can also use a recorder, who keeps the class diary, a short account of what is done each week, for ready reference and review. No treasurer is needed, as it is unwise or too complicated for children to handle money. (Note: If the "class treasury system" is used in your school, you will elect a treasurer, who keeps track of the money brought in or earned by the class, and who reports to the adult school treasurer the projects on which the class has voted to spend its money. This system assumes that the vestry pays for school expenses out of its budget, but allows the children to make their own decisions with respect to their class money.)

It is better to agree early how often to change officers. Some teachers decide to have an election once a month, some twice a year. This passes responsibility around, prevents any unworthy or difficult child from holding office too long, and gives several children the experience of leadership.

Have a short business session at the *close* of each class period. This is always a time-user, so agree to turn the meeting over to the president five minutes before the closing bell. Then the class can linger on their own time.

Most important of all, begin early the formation of a set of class rules, which shall define the mind and agreement of all. If you call for suggestions, the following are likely to be offered and to appear on the blackboard:

Do not chew gum.

Let one person talk at a time.

Always be on time for the opening.

Do not kick under the table.

Respect the rights of others.

Do not whisper in church (or: Set a good example to the younger children.)

Always find your place in the Hymnal and Prayer Book.

Be courteous, be friendly.

Do not tip back on hind legs of chairs.

This list, posted on the wall, is referred to frequently, amended by vote. Violators may be compelled (by popular demand) to read aloud the code. The list may be read in concert occasionally.

If the class chooses a name, selects a badge from some catalogue, and has a handshake and a password, then the teacher can feel sure of a good year ahead. His pupils are a class, a family, one "swell bunch."

30

Only Two Recited

YES, I watched your class and noticed that, too. Two of your children seemed to be answering all the questions—that boy and that girl. Sometimes it was only the girl. I could see that you were really trying at times to get some of the others to say something, that you often tried to get those two to put down their hands and desist.

This has been going on for a long time—from the very first meeting of your class, no doubt. At first perhaps it felt good to have such a ready response, to have all your questions answered so glibly. But in time you began to realize that it was a lopsided performance, with two stars and a silent chorus. You wonder if the policy to "work for response" has not degenerated into a slick performer's routine. What can be done about it?

Let's analyze the situation, which is far more general than most people realize, and see if we can find the reasons and perhaps some better ways.

Recall the familiar setting. You make some statement, then ask some open question calling for an obvious reply. Perhaps it is a question of fact, recalling matter from preceding lessons. The two remember it at once. If it was a question calling for opinion or meaning, they also seize the stage.

Is the teacher at fault? How were the questions worded and to whom addressed? Did you really want an answer or only an echo? If you will try to recall the manner in which you habitually phrase your questions, you may discover the reason. How did you offer them? Did you ask a general question, looking around for an answer? You know all too well who will hair-trigger the answer.

The first step is for the teacher to stop throwing out questions to the whole circle, in effect calling for eager volunteers. Instead, say: "I am aiming this next question at Suzanne. And we will wait until she can answer it."

What if Suzanne does not know or is embarrassed or silent? Say: "We'll let Suzanne think for a while. Perhaps she can look it up in the reader. Or she may wish to ask at home and report next Sunday. If anybody knows, please don't tell her!"

Another device is to provide questions typed on slips—a different one for each pupil—to be answered briefly in writing. They are judiciously chosen or designed to fit the needs of each recipient. Then the slips may be exchanged and the answers discussed.

The real problem behind the difficulty we are discussing lies in the fact that your pupils have not been made to look upon the class as a fellowship and to see that making a pert reply is not really playing the whole game. The bright ones may come to see that they have a special responsibility to help the slower ones. You may have to have a private talk with each star. They will often see the teacher's difficulty, that they are really being problems, and they may join the teacher and try to "help us make the other ones understand."

But deeper than securing their cooperation, there is a more serious personality problem with these two. The quick reciters often only *seem* the brightest. They have acquired a habit of quick response and have found satisfaction in their performance. They have confidence from past success, and they like it. In short, they are show-offs. The urge that makes an adult reveal private information and become a malicious gossip, may operate also in a child who, unconsciously craving approbation, tells what he knows. In the cases of the two pupils cited here mere performance has been made a substitute for real superiority and it can become a pattern in their lives.

It may well be that you have a duty to help your two pupils to see their quick speech as a weakness, not a virtue, and to find pleasure in other ways of self-expression. Other cures are given briefly:

(1) Follow up your stars' answers with: "Why do you think so?" "Are you sure?" By this time others in the class may see deeper meanings in the question. If a question is worth asking, it is worth expanding.

(2) Note the errors of your stars and call their attention to them. They are often guessing, rushing in without real thought.

(3) Use other ways of teaching, requiring various forms of pupil response—for example: silent reading and report from reader or Bible; writing of definitions, prayers, litany, even poems; simple role playing; or any kind of handwork allowing for differences of expression.

You can change this habit of your class if you work at it.

31

Let the Class Be a Class

ALL OF US, at any age, find refuge, comfort, and release by belonging to "our own class." Even the dream of a classless society yields to the human need for a peer group to which one truly belongs.

It is good to be in a class. You have support and companionship and feel secure. This is what children need. They tend to seek their own age group. (So do all of us, much of the time.) There they instinctively feel that they will find kindred spirits, equal competition, the same outlook and problems, the same needs and interests. It's more *fun* to be with your crowd.

The church school class, if kept small enough—say, under ten—can become a vital force in the lives of its members. But the teacher must first have a rich concept of the meaning of class, or group, fellowship. If he looks upon his pupils as only a *list of individuals* to be instructed, he will never have a class. The wise teacher works always to create and then use the awareness of personal relation of pupils to each other, and the whole to some high purpose.

What makes a class a class? Some of the conditions are ready at hand. We have familiarity and frequent meetings. Frankly, this is one of the main reasons for regular attendance—not that the absentee might miss a lesson, but that the class is weaker without his personal giving and receiving in the group life.

Shared responsibility unites a class. The secretary is not just appointed, but elected. Duties performed are done by the individual to fulfill the responsibility of the class as a whole—and, therefore, they should be done in rotation. "Our" class takes the offering or puts out the Bibles or straightens the books.

A good project unites a class. Next to the educational reason for carrying through a project, the unifying experience may be one of the main goals. First, there is an introductory discussion, the "warming-up," when individual notions jell in a common desire. Then in the planning, imaginations are stimulated, and the completed plan is felt to be "ours." Then the carrying-through, the making, doing, acting, selling, sending, and finally on through to the evaluating —"What did we learn by this?"—and the look into the future—"We can do it this way better next time."

Intercessory prayer helps make a class. The wise teacher proposes needy persons and causes and guides the group into common prayer for them. Classes have been known to keep prayer calendars for themselves and their families, to pray for sick or troubled persons who live in the parish or who are prominent in the news. Thus they can pray for a condemned man, for some sick child, for the peace of the world, et cetera. If they do not start to practice these things together as a class, when are they likely to learn them alone?

A good set of rules unites a class. When pupils have some share in formulating what they agree on as the character of their class, they will have a morale that transcends the usual vague obedience and saves the teacher from being a policeman. "We do it this way." "We speak one at a time." "We pick up our class table."

Above all—and in every session—good discussion makes a class a vital thing. This for any age is the mystery of human companionship, now revealed to us in the dawning science of group dynamics.

A class is a class when individuals *give themselves* to the common life. The talker must have an interested audience; talkers must also learn to listen. Every member must be in turn arrow, then target; actor, then critic; creator, then evaluator; leader, then follower; innovator and yet cooperator.

Is this too complicated? Then let's say simply: "In a class (or any group small enough to carry on a conversation) learning takes place from the give-and-take of personalities." This is Group Process.

Finally, the teacher must *join the class* if it is to be a class! He is still himself—an adult, informed, experienced, but mid-course in his own life. Yet he resigns, as nearly as he can, his old roles of disciplinarian, lecturer, instructor, and task master. He becomes one of a company of eager persons learning together.

32

The Church in Miniature

"IN EVERY Sunday school class we have a little world similar
to the life in the early Church." So an old priest of my ac-
quaintance once remarked. He added: "Every class contains
in miniature all the essentials of the life of the whole
Church."

He went on to elaborate this surprising assertion. "In the
class we have, first, frequent assembly of the same earnest,
believing people, as in apostolic times. They believed that
by their assembling ('two or three gathered in His name')
they achieved His Presence among them. There was intimate
fellowship on the most complete terms of equality. Finally,
there were recognized leaders with authority from the Head
to discipline (i.e., disciple), train, inspire, and send forth daily
on His mission."

He could have added that there was mutual concern, courtesy and assistance, and also a recognition of the personality
and contribution of each one. The groups in the early
Church were small, and they loved each other so evidently
that the world noted it. The Christian life was lived and
learned in company. It is an interesting analysis.

The New Testament shows the first Christians as a small
group of intimates who met frequently for prayer and mutual
support and to recall their experience of their Lord. (Notice

how the personal names of Christian brethren are found all through St. Paul's epistles.) Their evident custom of reciting for themselves and for newcomers the actions and words of the Lord gave rise to the collection of those fragments that a few years later became the Gospels. These were in reality the first curriculum, the working notes of the teaching Church. Their common life, from day to day, was filled with frequent mention of Jesus, whom they knew to be ever among them and involved in all their relations with one another. It has even been suggested by critics that they may have had a password or greeting in the Aramaic vernacular: *Maranatha* (if we interpret I Cor. 16:22 and the *Apostolic Constitutions*). It means "O Lord, come."

Today every class in our schools—if all is well—continues these conditions. There is regular assembly, certainty of the Presence, and the expression of rich fellowship and love. And, as of old, there is the chosen mature leader, literally the "elder." Everything is there. All of them are already Christians, though with a long way yet to go. As the class lives its life, there is the steady process of learning the Faith as they grow older year by year together.

Our class is, then, a cell of the whole, a sample in perfect miniature. If we teachers strive to make our classes into such a pattern, we may attain the same rich life of the early Church. Could we from now on take our working ideal, our mental picture of what we are doing, from this grand idea? This will involve teaching the tradition and lore as heretofore—but also very much more. It will include the teacher's serious attempt to serve as a guide in worship. It will mean the recognition of the group's experience of common prayer through sharing in subjects for intercession. There will be stimulation and guidance in the arts of meditation and of profitable Bible reading.

With this clue the teacher recognizes himself as the pastor of his little flock, responsible that not one of them be lost. It will mean that the teacher puts first, not lessons, but experiences. He will strive to create a friendly group, worshiping, studying, praying, singing, playing, traveling, searching together. He will break up all conditions and trends that undermine its tone and quality.

In such a world every person will be of importance, and his problems the concern of the teacher. There will be the observance of birthdays. There may even be formal letters as special needs arise—truly pastoral letters, as important to the local need as any of Saint Paul's.

It will take more time, for in reality the class will be continuous. The fellowship will have no break, but its members will be thinking its thoughts and living its plans and projects every day of the week. There will be, too, the study and use of the sacraments in the larger circle of the parish.

One first step toward this new way would be to promote within the class intimate discussion of the real reasons for being churchmen and what "our" class should be doing. Once any group recognizes its possibilities and its true character, it can begin to live its full life. Your class will become the Church in sample, in action. You will be the Church.

PART IV

The New Objectives

THE LADDER OF
Learning

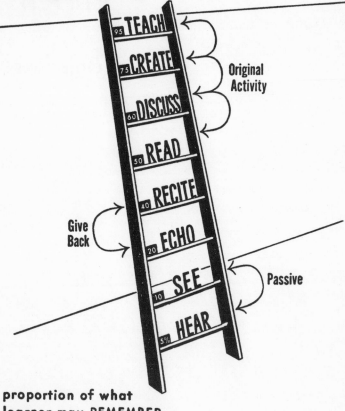

The proportion of what
the learner may REMEMBER
ALWAYS is shown by the %
given on each step

33

The Best Way to Learn

A FAIR test of your education is how much remains with you through life. This applies to religious, as well as general, education. In the church school, planned for children and youths, how can we be sure that the experiences we offer will be permanent, deep, and for life? The test for the learning of purely factual matter is whether it can be remembered years afterward. Perhaps more important in religion than factual recall, there are those standards, attitudes, habits, and emotional patterns which were well started in childhood and are still operating in adult life. Such a person has been well taught. Or perhaps it would be more accurate to say that his *learning* experiences have changed him permanently.

Our sketch shows the experiences in organized schooling by which learning is stimulated, guided, and accomplished. Teachers employ these ways according to their skill and knowledge of the arts of teaching. Some teachers use only one or two; others know how to adapt all of them from time to time to fit differing goals of teaching. On a single day several of these methods may be utilized. The day's theme or the pupils' age level or past lessons may cause a single one to be stressed almost exclusively. The training and educational philosophy of the teacher will also determine which methods are used.

Which of the following eight ways of learning is best? They are arranged here in an ascending scale of value. Our test is: How much does the pupil learn in a way that will last for life? Which way or ways will make such an impression that the things learned will be remembered and used always? Note that in this analysis the *learning* process is described. *Teaching* will be devised to provide these learning experiences.

(1) *Hearing* in the classroom is the most common and yet the lowest level of experience. This is to say that *telling* (lecturing, explaining, instructing, preaching, or reading aloud from a book) makes little permanent impression. Without some way of response, the spoken words of the teacher are not long retained. They are, indeed, "gone with the wind." By this method, the teacher, using his voice, gives factual information in the presence of the class. Personal warmth and a touch of emotion may enhance the effect, but there is still only speaker and audience. Unhappily, the largest part of our traditional teaching in the church school is carried on by this method. The untrained teacher knows scarcely any other way.

(2) *Seeing* enhances hearing and quite often accompanies it. The gestures and facial expressions of the teacher may help, particularly if he knows how to look directly at his pupils and catch every eye. Add pictures, charts, blackboard to the teacher's words, and you have the much-advertised "audio-visual education." We see this in its most inflated form in television. Flip the switch and you are bathed in an everflowing stream of sight and sound. How much is remembered? Does it make any permanent impression?

In the church school this combination of sound and sight has been utilized mainly through projected pictures—the grandchild of the old magic lantern. We project slides, filmstrips, and movies. In addition, we use flannelgraphs, printed pictures of all sorts, and our old faithful blackboard—now frequently displaced by the newsprint pad. In both steps (1) and (2) it should be realized that, although the pictures and the talk may be greatly improved, these still make little permanent impression, because the pupil is passive and inactive.

(3) *Echoing* is the playback of the teacher's own words. The teacher gives a summarizing phrase, saying: "Class, repeat!" Sometimes an individual is called upon to repeat. Again, prescribed questions and answers may be employed, and the pupils required to use these until they can give them back exactly. This is the catechetical method, with its authoritative wording, which dominated the educational field for centuries in the Church. From the point of view of the Church's leaders, this may have been justified as a means of preserving the Faith without error from generation to generation. It took little account of childhood needs, of changing phraseology, and of vital learning. We still have the catechism, now modified into the Offices of Instruction, as well as some privately prepared catechisms of exact verbal summaries of what it is thought the well-trained Christian ought to know. These have value as carefully prepared compendiums of theology and may be of use to teachers as a check on their own grasp of the Faith. The logical and systematic arrangement of these catechisms may help in planning lessons, too. But as the end purpose of Christian education these are now recognized to have far less value for life than some of the activity methods that follow. Thousands of people now living will never know the catechism, but they may become informed Christians by other means.

It should be noted that echoing is not to be confused with *memorizing* selected passages from the Bible—hymns, psalms, and prayers for devotional use throughout life. These might be classed as aspects of personal skill in employing the treasures of the Church's culture. By "echoing" we mean here simply the effort to secure response by calling only for exact repetition of set words. A teacher of the youngest children often does this under the impression that he is giving them a vocabulary or at least helping them to say something when they are too immature to have original answers. This is, indeed, a kind of response, but of little value for remembering.

(4) *Reciting* in your own words is the beginning of original participation. Recitation is sometimes spoken, sometimes written. Until you can *put something into your own words* you have not really grasped it. The finding of words to express what has been perceived is at the heart of all learning. Some ideas may be too difficult to express readily, and other ways than words may have to be found, but the effort to express ideas for yourself results in true learning, and this will last. The finding of ways to *restate* the prescribed lesson first given by the teacher is the experience at this level. Later, at step (6), personal expression will be achieved in relation to a *group*.

This step and the following ones may be considered varieties of self-expression. They often interweave, so that the pupil employs now one, now another. The use of words in many forms is basic to all human relations and communication. Many of our pupils will never be able to express themselves brilliantly, but nearly everyone can be original— that is, do it in his own way—and it is our privilege as teachers to lead them to this life-giving experience. The theme of religion, dealing with the inmost matters of the heart and involving all our motives, supremely calls for self-expression. Therefore, teachers, help your pupils to start saying or doing things in their own way. This is how we grow into persons.

(5) *Reading* requires effort and concentration. You either keep on reading or put down the book—or fall asleep. If you are reading for a purpose, as when making a report or for teaching others, you have the added effort of interpretation and rephrasing in your own words *for someone else*. Reading takes us directly to the minds of others. It helps us

share in the accumulated treasures of our culture, and vastly widens the resources of the classroom. Reading by the pupil is employed in our church teaching both in the class and at home from about the fourth grade on. The teacher's encouragement to do research and report can make reading a rich part of religious education. In school and throughout life we acquire much of our knowledge from the printed page. The act of reading is voluntary and a personal achievement. It therefore makes a deeper, more lasting impression.

(6) *Discussion* is a high level of learning experience when planned and guided well. This is the area of the so-called group dynamics. Today we more often speak of discussion as conversation with a purpose. There are three factors involved in a good discussion, and if all three are operative, there will be an intense and permanent way of learning. These are: (a) The *individual* participant, who is stimulated to find expression for his own vague ideas in ways new to him and in areas of thought that he has not entered before. Or he may be helped to clarify his present ideas by conflict and adjustment to others. (b) The *theme,* or problem, stated by the leader or chosen by the group, which is developed freely through the stages of definition and clarification, conflict, personal adjustment, conclusion or decision, and, frequently, action. (c) The *group,* to which the individual willingly gives himself, using it first for audience, then support, and finally for sharing and fellowship. The rise of a better understanding of the group marks a new day in education, and this experience is wonderfully suited to religious education.

Throughout this book the experience of group life is shown with many variations. The Sunday morning class may become a group. When a class truly becomes a group—not just a captive audience for the teacher's talk—then a quality of learning may be experienced which will surely sink deeper and last longer than any of the preceding levels.

(7) Come up one more step. You have not really accom-

plished anything yet, you have only played with words. *Doing* is necessary for learning. When a teacher skillfully provides a way (or contrives to stimulate us to find a way) to express a theme in some physical form, it strikes deeply into us, and much of it will last forever. We are a part of all that we have done, and our achievements have made us. In the school laboratory we learn by going through each experiment for ourselves—not by merely watching the instructor perform it. We learn by drawing, making, performing. This may include writing, for this is a physical effort, with a finished product. In the teaching of religion, creative writing may include prayers, hymns, poems, litanies, letters, and definitions. Pupils may turn to any or all of the arts—acting, singing, modeling, painting. In worship, too, we use our bodies as well as our minds. The lower steps are an approach, but this is learning that will be with us forever.

To illustrate how, in one or two sessions, an ordinary class might use all of the seven steps described above, consider the following brief account: A fifth-grade class was to see a filmstrip on the Good Samaritan. The teacher first briefly explained what was to be shown, describing the scene with our Lord and the lawyer (step 1). The filmstrip was shown, with a script and some impromptu remarks (step 2). The teacher then asked the class to identify the principal characters and to answer, in the words of the parable: "Which was neighbor?" (step 3). Next, various children were asked to describe or to give their reaction to a particular point in the filmstrip (step 4). They then took up their Bibles and silently read the original story, after being asked to look for any points added to, or left out of, the filmstrip (step 5).

The following Sunday the group carried on the theme in a developed discussion, starting with the teacher's stating that it's hard to be a neighbor to people you have never seen. The class soon raised points of their own and wanted, toward the end, to do something helpful—perhaps for some local family or institution. This was the group (step 6). On the third Sunday this class completed plans for a trip to an old people's home, taking them treats and singing for them (step 7).

(8) Some experts in pedagogy would leave the matter here —with activity as the high point of learning. You might say that when the pupil has learned by hearing, seeing, echoing, reciting, reading, discussing, and doing he has received all that the learning process can offer him. Yet there is one step even higher. Let me introduce you to the topmost step by a familiar parable.

A young man, about to flunk his senior year at college, wrote home, admitting the sad fact to his father and mentioning also that he might yet pass if he could be tutored intensively. His father wired: "Get the best tutor. Spare no expense." Whereupon the boy asked his adviser to recommend the best tutor on the campus.

The adviser made the classic reply: "Tutor? Get a pupil!"

This is a truth too little appreciated. Teachers know the most because they have had to prepare for teaching. And teachers remember the most because they are the most involved in the complete process of teaching. Teachers must master their subject, not for personal interest, nor to pass a school test, but to give it to others. And in so preparing and then teaching, they must know their pupils and all their needs, limitations, and possibilities. Teachers gradually grow to meet the demand that people are to be taught, not just subject matter. For many people, the call to do some form of teaching is the only motive for learning, once schooldays are past. You never really know something until you have tried to pass it on to someone else—in a form that can be grasped by your students and with an enthusiasm that will send them on to make their own discoveries.

The moral for us in the Church? For teachers, let your pupils do some of the teaching. Visit any public school and see how a child stands before the class and conducts a drill. For the clergy, make it your constant purpose to see that as many of your people as possible be given the transforming experience of teaching. For teaching is the best way to learn.

This, then, is our Ladder of Learning, shown in the drawing. You will climb up and down its rungs many times as you practice the arts of teaching. To add some meaning, we venture to suggest a percentage for each step. This is not based on any tests or research. It is the writer's own estimate of *what proportion of the matter studied* will be most likely to be *remembered* through life. Make your own estimates if you will, but see the ascending values of the different forms of learning. You will use all of them in your class; use the higher ones more often.

Our estimate: People (of all ages) may remember 5% of what they hear, 10% of what they see, 20% of what they repeat, 40% of what they say in their own words, perhaps 50% of what they read, 60% of what they discuss in a vital group, 75% of what they do or make, and fully 95% of what they teach.

34

A Working Formula

IT IS clear by now that if we are to train teachers in the newer ways of religious education, we must have some means of helping them to see clearly the contrast with the older ways. Older teachers (and older persons who are not teachers) have a fixed conception of the aim and procedures of Christian teaching. Mainly their minds conceive of class teaching in this order: (1) Present the material for the lesson. (2) Explain it. (3) Drill on the facts and the declared meaning. (4) Give application to life.

Since the interest and effort center mainly in the material (generally a narrative portion from the Bible) and since the lesson time has nearly run out, the last point is usually covered by a few stock admonitions, with little effort to discover the children's real concerns.

This summary is, indeed, a caricature, but it is stated to show the contrast with the new order. The new way, on the whole, reverses the order completely, or at least it completely alters the focus of attention of the teacher. We now have as a typical procedure the following: (1) Raise a problem or going concern of the pupils; let them express this in their own words, and allow the group to share. (2) Let some practical, *human* solutions be proposed, although not dogmatically or finally. (3) Direct this aroused concern toward one or more *religious* solutions, already partially known or at hand. (4) Allow or stimulate some original *expression* of this in project activity.

The old order worked from lore to life, or tried to. Proofs are mounting that this was not largely successful. The new order moves from life as it is now being lived toward meanings and solution in the Christian religion. We literally bring people (as they are) to Christ (who is in the Church).

Our pupils—all of us, indeed—are in a certain place *now*. We are in the mid-current of our lives, at any age. There is a future, but we must solve today's problems. If we are to help people, we must know how to guide them in their next steps. They are more sure of where they are than of where they should go next. In Ligon's vivid phrase, "Their future is now." They need help, because their problem baffles them.

Along the line of such thoughts a working formula is here offered for the planning of a lesson period.

The theory: That all human problems find their solution, and their only final solution, in Christ and the Church.

The formula for a lesson following this theory has four steps, as outlined above:

(1) Locate a present concern or problem common to the group, and allow its expression in the pupils' own language. (This is a new teaching area and calls for new skills in the art of questioning and probing. These are given in this book.)

(2) "What can we do about it?" Allow children to propose possible ways of dealing with the problem. This is the way of human solution, and may result in the discovery that the problem is pretty big, and nothing much can be done about it. By having everyone share the problem, they all see it as a common human predicament.

(3) Steer the talk toward a *religious* solution. This may emerge earlier than expected and may be in the pupils' own

124

terms. "Does God care about this?" "Can we find an answer from Him?" "Do you remember anything we have learned in the Bible? In our worship?" These and similar questions are used to point the conversation. (Here and elsewhere the inner secret of the new teaching is: Don't *tell* them too much. Hold back. Ask questions of opinion, not of fact.)

(4) Finally, when someone has suggested a resource and the thought is headed toward a religious answer, the leader may clinch it with a Scripture incident or passage. This may have been determined in advance or may come from the teacher's mental store, suggested by the discussion. Attention may be drawn to some item in church life—some service, collect, hymn, or sentence. Curiously, we are finding that at this stage in a well-managed session pupils will themselves suggest such matters. If not, the teacher will; but such references are best when made to points already partially known or observed. Here is the advantage of having children attend a liturgical service with their parents, instead of the watered-down children's service of the past. Then they become steeped in normal church life, and in class find meanings for it.

There are other variations in the application of this new approach, but the foregoing will serve to point to the contrast with the old. Some ways of varying this are given in the following chapter.

35

Lore and Concern

MOST TEACHERS are now aware of the distinction between "lore" and "concern." At least they will have heard these two terms used at meetings and in articles about the new approach. In case their full meaning is not clear, let's examine both words and see what they mean.

Years of child study have made us see that, unless we understand our pupils, we cannot start them learning. We now go deeper and ask: "What are our children thinking?" "What is really on their minds?" "What are their small worries, their unspoken questions?" "What is the real world of day-to-day thought in which they live?" This is far more than the former child study, in which we described the conduct of typical children in each year of their lives. This is getting beneath the surface, getting in touch with the real child, whose outward conduct might still hide his actual concerns. The old approaches may be the cause of the many news stories of a "model" child who does some unexpected and frightful thing.

Thus was written on the educational blackboard the new word—*concern*. It is important that we understand clearly all that is meant by it, lest it be accepted as a word only, used by the newcomer glibly but without full appreciation of its scope. We are now using the term *concern* to refer to the present content of our pupils' minds. We say, in the greeting phrase of the street: "What's on your mind?" and we partly mean it. To meet a person, you must contact his present awareness, the things that are in the forefront of his mind at the moment. More particularly, we hope to discover the matters that are felt deeply, about which a person is really troubled or elated or bewildered—in short, the things with which he is now concerned, whether he talks freely about them or not.

What is *lore?* We now use the word to mean knowledge of the Church from the past. It is sometimes called *heritage*—what we have received from our spiritual ancestors and must hand on to our children. From this concept comes the traditional educational theory of transmission, or handing-on. The things that may be included under lore are numerous, and adults are broadly aware of them. Lore includes everything in the Bible and Prayer Book, also church history, customs and practices, and the settled formulas of the Faith. These things our children should know, we feel sure.

Clearly, both lore and concern are important. We must find a way to touch concern; we must give our pupils a working knowledge of their inheritance of Christian lore. But how can we do both?

In brief, the following four ways of dealing with these seemingly opposed areas may be used by teachers. On a given Sunday here are the possibilities:

(1) *Deal with nothing but lore.* That is, present a Bible passage, incident, or experience as the "lesson," simply as something to be learned. It might be impressed by drill, but no effort need be made at the time to interpret. Simply present the facts and their current details. You *tell* them. You *explain* as clearly as you can. This is fairly easy; some teachers do it always, and often nothing else.

(2) *Start with lore, but end with concern.* For example, give a Bible incident, ending it with an application to present

127

life. This ending easily degenerates into a neat little moral lecture by the teacher, most often stressing helpfulness and kindness and seldom anything else; but it can be vital if original expression is desired and started. This is the classic form of the Bible lesson that held the field for a hundred years or more, and conservative teachers now find it difficult to abandon for other ways. It is the order of most of our sermons—that is, Bible text expounded, then applied.

(3) *Deal with nothing but concern.* Here the teacher aims, by probing questions or by loosely guided conversation, to draw out the feelings and interests of his pupils. At its worst, this plan may be all-out progressive education; at its best, it is a preliminary to guided learning in a later session. Often it is a means of welding the class into a solid *group,* in which real learning may begin to take place.

(4) *Start with concern, but end with lore.* For example, start a conversation on the things we are afraid of, leading into shared ideas of trust in God and where we can find a collect to help. (This is the procedure given in more detail in the preceding chapter.)

Note that plans (1) and (2) are in the old style. They are still workable and necessary at times, but they do not make use of the new discoveries in vital teaching. Plans 3 and 4 start with concern and are used by teachers who genuinely believe that we must touch the hidden springs of life before we can hope to impart any knowledge. It is not merely that we are to get our pupils started and in motion toward the old mass of subject matter; rather, we hope to serve our children as they are, using what portions of lore are applicable. (Certainly they can never know all of the lore!)

Teachers may plan a lesson on any one of the four ways above, but they should never fall into the habit of using any one exclusively.

36

Some New Problems

Now THAT an increasing number of teachers are using the new approach in the church school, it is valuable for a group of them to get together and compare notes. The following is a short report of a workshop that was conducted for teachers who had been using one of the newer series of texts for a period of from two months to a year. The leader of the workshop, himself skilled in the ways of group-life meetings, first made the forty teachers at ease by some quick introductions, including the name of their parish and some facts about each.

Then he posed this question: "Now that you have been teaching one of the new courses for some time, what problem or difficulty have you encountered? Let's compare notes and try to solve them."

Various problems or perplexities were mentioned and listed on the paper-board. These formed the agenda of the meeting, which lasted with undiminished interest for nearly three hours. Following are some of the problems listed briefly. After each are the comments and suggestions made by the group.

(1) How to "draw pupils out." Agreed that this means to get at the child's own ideas, not merely to pump until you get what you think is the right answer.

(2) How to prevent a child "from talking too much." This is often the smart child who jumps to the "right" answer too soon, spoiling the teacher's planned build-up. It includes also the talkative child who has not learned to listen and who needs to feel the interplay of group life. He really wants attention. He may require a personal conference outside of the class period.

(3) "How to keep on the track." You must know your goal for the year and not be disturbed by temporary digressions.

These first three points are related to the whole problem of developing new skill in the control of conversation—how to be permissive and drive with a loose rein, but with a steady purpose.

(4) *When* do they learn? What is learning? Is it to be exposed to information spoken aloud, or is it memorizing words? Or is it the deep impression made on a life and its bent, not measurable now?

(5) "They thought I was crazy"—for telling an open-end story. But later they caught on to the idea and loved it. This is a good sign that the teacher felt the contrast with the old methods and was alert to the responses of the class. She was learning by trial and observation.

(6) Individual needs of pupils. A need was felt for taking notes on each child. It was felt that we now have an awareness more of persons and their needs than of organized information.

(7) Home life revealed by a child's remarks and conduct. Can we do anything about this? Need for other contacts than Sunday—parish life and activities of all kinds. Teachers calling at the homes, and regular intercessions for every child —dealing with the full life of everyone.

(8) What if the teacher doesn't know the answer? Shall we be anxious to save face as the "wise one," or are we willing to become companions? It developed that most of the teachers had in mind questions of fact (to which the reply can

always be given: "Let's look it up"), whereas children's questions tended to be mostly about meanings and interpretations —the why and how. Further, children's so-called questions may not call for an answer in full or in great depth; they may be only symptoms of some interest vaguely felt, with no ready means known by the child to express it. Frequently it can be turned over to the child by saying: "What do *you* think about it?"

(9) How to begin each session. Attention was called to some good examples in the printed texts. Many a start is suggested by last week's conversation or devised in the conference between teacher and observer.

(10) "There do not seem to be any goals." Such a teacher is still in the grip of the opinion that you must come to each class armed and determined to "teach them *something*," by which is usually meant information, narrative matter, or a verbalized summary. The year's goals, it was pointed out, are clearly stated in each text and developed variously through the year.

(11) "There is no lesson for each Sunday." There is none in the public school either. The class continues from session to session in a developing stream of interest in one theme.

(12) "Is this a guessing game?" Some teachers felt that to defer "telling" the children would cause them to start figuring out "what the teacher is aiming at," and this would be as authoritarian as the old ways. But if the teacher will not drive so hard, will learn to play up and develop the ideas of pupils, they will express themselves more freely.

(13) "Will there be permanent results?" Habits developed in a loving circle of parish and home, with acceptance of each person as he is for what he is, must be permanent. All talking and action carried on with earnest desire and inward motivation will be a part of us always. (See problem 4.)

(14) "Where does the Bible come in?" Sometimes as the answer to a dilemma. Sometimes as direct resource. Some-

times as golden portions of the Church's literature to be memorized for pleasure and for devotional use.

The leader of this workshop acted only as stimulator and moderator, and at the end gave a swift summary, adding some points not mentioned. The teachers provided most of the material and conclusions. Yet they undoubtedly *learned* far more than if the same matter had been given in the form of a lecture by one expert. They had seen and taken part in a group experience, with needs discovered and solutions proposed. It had been for them a *demonstration* of the way in which they will apply the new approach in their own classes.

37

Information Plus

To MAKE more clear the meaning of lore, or heritage, we might examine its typical presentation. When teachers plan a review for the purpose of revealing what their pupils have learned, they ask for a playback of the matter recently covered in class. In so doing, and especially in the way they arrange the review, they reveal their own conception of their objectives. *This* is what they have been trying to accomplish, and they are now checking up on themselves.

If you could read the examination questions prepared by many teachers, you would soon discover that they deal almost exclusively with *information*. In desiring to check on the accomplishment of their pupils, these teachers seemed to think that the most important things for their children to know permanently were the correct names of certain Bible characters and the incident connected with each, a few stock facts and pat definitions, a key date, and how to identify certain key words. Nearly all of these facts were very obvious and easy and would have been retained by anyone who had attended even a few of the class sessions. Nothing was asked about the children's reactions, attitudes, interpretations.

A little exploration revealed that the textbooks used by these teachers were almost exclusively devoted to such information. No wonder the teachers considered this their main duty in teaching. The distorted emphasis was in the minds of the writers, and behind *them* in turn, the same obsession in the approach of the editorial board that had mapped the over-all scheme for the entire series of courses. These things "must" be taught—some in first grade, others in second, and so on—and the title of the course was framed to suggest the theological aim: "The Ten Commandments." By such planning, religious education comes to mean mainly the imparting of a mass of information about the Christian religion. It might be made more interesting by various devices, but "these things they should know."

To be fair, the texts did mention other teaching points—a memory item, a prayer, or even an outcome to be discussed, but these were seldom stressed by the teachers and were felt to be only appendages to the lesson. The result of such an emphasis is that there is a monotonous sameness about many church school classes. It is boring to the pupils and, I often suspect, to the teachers. Here we go again: "Take the roll. . . . Hunt up the class box. . . . Where are the pencils? . . . Put away that comic book! . . . Review. . . . Who were the sons of Isaac? . . . Now let's have it quiet. . . . The lesson today is about Jacob's dream. . . . If you're not quiet, I won't go on with the story. . . . And there were thousands of angels. . . . Application—there are always angels near us. . . . Quiet. . . . Quiet. . . . Now open your workbooks. The first blank is . . . Let me look it up. . . . *Bethel*. . . . Have you all written that? . . . Now the true-false list. . . ." Facts, facts, information, names, words, words . . .

The cure? It may not be as easy as we would like, because the disease is deep-seated, and the patients are scarcely aware that they are ill. *This* is "religious" education! What do you expect? Charm? Fun? "If those other classes would be more quiet . . ." "If we could have a better textbook . . ." And so it goes.

Now to put the finger on one great weakness, the conception of teaching above can be blamed on the notion that the imparting of information is the main thing. Facts are the lowest level of knowledge, and the easiest to teach. But unless they are functional, they are as barren as a skeleton; that is, unless they are made to live, the neatest collections of facts are only dry bones.

Teachers need to grasp the concept of the diversity and wide range of Christian knowledge and the need to give proportion in their teaching in every lesson. There are, indeed, five areas with which every church teacher should be dealing. These are: (1) Information—important in relation to the whole, but not the most important. (2) Church loyalty —how and why churchmen behave; this should be dealt with in detail, and practiced and drilled a little every Sunday. (3) Devotional life—personal religion, attitudes and habits of prayer and worship; this should be started at church and guided at home. (4) Memorizing literary gems of the Faith, to be used for the enrichment of life through the years. (5) Most of all, vital conversation and expressive activity by means of which the resources of the Christian faith are related to the problems of present living. Some of this will start in class, but we must see that more of it occurs in daily living.

This, then, is the cure for a class, a course, or a series that is afflicted with "informationitis": Weave something of the five topics above into every course and, if possible, into *every lesson*. Each topic will be discovered to be a large subject, to be broken up into smaller details. If a teacher seeks to get *something of all five* into every lesson, things will be different.

38

The Blight of Verbalism

ALL TYPES of teaching and learning make use of words to convey ideas. Words are the easiest and commonest form of human mental intercourse. But therein lies their danger: the speaker is never quite sure that his words give to his hearers the meaning that he intended. Or, rather, many people speak their piece and feel confident that this is enough. "I told them," is their feeling.

Teachers must work always in some manner with words. But the obsession with words for their own sake may easily steal upon us. The difficulty comes from confusing the end with the process. Somewhere somebody gets a new idea. He expresses it in his own words. He tries out his definitions on his friends. In the process of stating and restating the main idea he keeps boiling it down to shorter and shorter phrases. Finally he reaches a crystallized formula, intelligible to his own circle.

The circle repeats the formula frequently; they know just what it means, for they have been through the process of finding words for their idea. Their terms may become common coin in the current issues of their professional journals, known to the initiated—and indeed repeated glibly and with pride by the lesser ones. "This is it," they think.

But this is not it. The newly discovered idea is greater than any words. If it is true, it can be stated in a thousand ways. If it can be stated only in a few trick words, it is probably not true.

So the Christian religion comes to us partly through words. However, it came to us across the years through translations into many languages. Because it is the truth, it can be stated in a thousand ways. At one period the Church, living through the learning process of understanding its faith, formulated a boiled-down summary which we know as "the Creed"—or rather "the creeds," for you can state the Faith several ways. The Creed comes to us, then, as the approved discovery of our ancestors. We use it as a convenient teaching formula.

But the creeds are not the Christian religion. They are only the graduation theses of students in past years.

What an experience it might be if all of us and our children could go through the process of personal discovery, then of finding words for its expression, and finally of having to find words (and ways) of conveying the discovery to others. That is teaching. Yet verbalism takes the place of real teaching everywhere.

The catechism is a form of verbalism. We drill on definitions, thinking we are giving our pupils the reality. But, like the Creed, these definitions are the end result of the thinking of others, of another generation who went through the process and found words.

Academic clichés are a form of verbalism. The inside coterie develops a jargon of words with special meaning, but finds that it only mystifies or annoys outsiders. Lesser pupils learn to repeat the new terms, but they grasp only dimly the inner lore. Fortunately the newer textbooks are being carefully edited to express ideas with crystal simplicity, devoid of jargon.

The echoed last word is rank verbalism. Thus, a teacher drills: "And if we are all good boys and girls, we will all go to . . . ?"

"Heaven!" shout the tots dutifully. We actually overheard this recently. And it occurs frequently in one form or another in the methods of teachers with strong personalities, who rely too much on words.

Reading in concert from the textbook or even from the Bible is likely to be verbalism, unless a way is found to vitalize it in the teaching. But to *tell* them what it *means* may just be more verbalism.

The use of big words, to which many people are addicted, is verbalism. Who can tell such self-conscious people that they neither impress nor transmit clear ideas?

"But," you say in exasperation, "if not words—what?"

All right, let's try to find the answer.

39

If Not Words—What?

THE NEW and vital way of teaching, whether religion or any-thing else, is a program of planned experience. It's very sim-ple once you get your mind off the trick formula, the inher-ited shibboleth. When you ask yourself: "What is the Chris-tian religion and how can I transmit it to anyone else?" you begin to think of real life—real people with present problems and interests.

Planned experience—but how? We shall not go to the ex-treme of imposing our iron purposes on our pupils. This is paternalism—just as bad as verbalism, for it looks upon the learner as something to be manipulated. The experience we plan shall be, so far as we can manage, appropriate for each pupil.

"I want my child," said a mother, "to go through all the right, developing experiences at each period in his life—the experiences that will form his character."

The tools or methods by which we shall guide children into these experiences are inherent in the Church's life. They are:

(1) Activities that develop skills. Just as every trade or art has its basic exercises, so does the Christian religion. These include such things as devotional habits and methods, how to

find your place in the Bible and the Prayer Book, memorizing prayers and golden passages for lifelong use, and the folk customs of family and parish.

(2) Expression through activities that are given symbolic or imaginative meaning. This means simply that what we do in class has a purpose. We make a drawing to express our idea of the story. We dramatize a narrative so that we may enter into the feelings of the characters. We make presents for the hospital in order to practice loving service.

(3) Original expression encouraged through all the known forms of artistic performance. Let the dancers dance and the singers sing, each in his own way, but in happy fellowship with the class. Here we may use words, but they are original words—definitions, prayers, poems, essays, letters. Or music —singing, playing, choosing, composing, listening. And physical activity—serving, acting, making.

(4) Opportunities for making choices. We shall provide sample situations from our day's experience and allow time for judgment and decision. This will lead to the sharing of opinions and, through that, to the discovery of standards.

We may start today's lesson with an anecdote from life, a challenge to serve, or the practice of a skill. But always we study the full rich tide of the Christian life into which we hope to launch our pupils. We may start with a picture, but we end with hunting some Bible clue. We may start with planning to help a missionary, but we end by finding what Christ said. Always we start where we are, then steer toward truths that are greater than words.

Instead of set words, we shall try to lead our pupils into religion with meaning.

40

Lecture or Discuss

THE ART of classroom discussion, or guided conversation, is today an accepted technique of our teaching, and its values and uses should be appreciated. In discussion everyone may be given an opportunity to express himself. This is in contrast to lecturing or telling, in which the teacher is the sole speaker. The following are some conclusions concerning the superiority of the discussion over the lecture method.

(1) Things learned through class discussion are remembered better and recalled at a much later period. Points received merely by telling may linger for a day or so or until the review or examination. Or isolated items may be retained, and the rest forgotten. Things discussed in the group, with the pleasure of participation, and in one's own vocabulary, are likely to be a part of us for life. Things discussed intelligently are better understood, sink in deeper, and last longer. They have *meaning*.

(2) The discussion method fits all levels of intelligence. The brilliant have scope for their original ideas, the average participate rather than merely conform, and the slow are found to grasp something, too, although they may not shine in the talking. Everybody is drawn into the discussion in a well-guided group, and all profit.

(3) The instructional, or lecture, method, on the other hand, favors the superior child. With his larger store of knowledge he can assimilate more new ideas, and with his quicker mind he will respond and restate more frequently. This has been the unequal situation under the old telling routine (which those of us who actually observe teaching can affirm): the one or two bright children in the class get the story quickly, make the desired replies—and then become a discipline problem.

(4) When individual *action* is to follow the teaching, the discussion method is far more effective. If you *tell* them what to do, they *may* do it. But if you have a free discussion of "How shall we do it?" the details will be better grasped, more original ideas will emerge, and all will get to work more heartily and happily. This is both communication and motivation which will benefit the entire class.

(5) The lecture, or telling, method misses almost entirely the values of the *group*. The teacher—a remote and detached adult behind a desk—sounds off in the presence of a number of separate *individuals*, seated in straight rows. Yet the *class* may become our best tool once it is galvanized into a group (of which the teacher is a fellow member).

"But," says the teacher who looks upon his role as that of Bearer of Information, "how can they ever know if I don't tell them?"

Let's face that issue. First, this type of teacher really believes that the Christian religion consists of a great body of information ("facts, truths, duties, rules, rubrics, and fundamentals," he may call them) which must be lodged in each oncoming young Christian. How? "By instructing him."

Second, the sheer quantity of this store of lore is so great that no seminary course can equip our clergy with it and a life of study does not master it all. For one thing, this mass not only has accumulated from the past, but is vitally alive in the present. If there is so much, it is clear that we cannot hope to give each pupil more than a small part of it.

Third, in our emerging modern view, the Faith is—and always has been—a living experience, worked out in the Christian community. It is what we do as Christians, among Christians, that makes us well-educated Christians. This is the exact meaning of "Christian nurture"—growth guided by people concerned and informed.

Fourth, let us freely admit that the discussion method is preliminary. But it is a vital form of the learning process. Into minds prepared, a few of the right seeds of the Gospel are planted. I estimate that under the new way of teaching, about 95 per cent of the classtime will be used for discussion, planning, working, visiting, research, and other expressive activities. Only about 5 per cent of the time will be devoted to telling, informing, instructing.

Therefore, it will take more time. The new ways are more profitable, but more leisurely. The teacher who now tells the story, reviews the facts swiftly, then spars for tricks to fill up the remaining twenty minutes, will be totally lost in the new approach—unless he takes the trouble to perfect himself in the ways of childhood and the guided conversation.

41

Self-Expression

To EXPRESS oneself in words is indeed normal. For if we are
to communicate with others, we must use the available means
of communication. But true self-expression is not the same
as "playback." Our children are not tape-recording machines;
they are persons.

"Self-expression" means that you are a person in your own
right, with a personality different from all others, and that
you have found a way to express that personality. We are all
like black bags containing strange treasures. To bring these
into the light will be our act of self-expression. It will require
groping and inward discovery. And the joy of bringing them
out is one of life's richest experiences.

A large part of our new educational aim consists in helping pupils find ways of expressing themselves. Some of them
are overstimulated, we realize—at least in respect to their
flow of words. They talk often and in many cases make no
great sense. Talking is their main outlet. For such pupils we
teachers need to provide a variety of other ways of expression.
We must also help them to deepen their expressiveness
through speech. The great problem is to motivate more of
our children to *some* sort of expression. Perhaps they were
thwarted, crushed at some stage. More possibly they were

never led to feel the satisfaction of achievement. The aim of the new guidance is not to steer the child into the teacher's pattern, but to let him be himself, his full self.

If you are one who feels antagonistic when you hear someone say, "That's progressive education," you should realize that this outlook dominates our thought today and that we can never go back to the old, stiff ways of authoritarian teaching.

Says progressive education: The child has a right to live richly, to have all the varied and beautiful experiences of which human life is capable. For that we must provide an environment rich enough to draw him out, and in which he can find himself.

We can assure the critics that the new, flexible ways of teaching religion are not "just progressive education, mere Deweyism." They do make large use of freedom and personal expression, but with this supreme difference: we carry on our teaching *within the ordered life of the Church.*

We do not stimulate our children to unrestricted self-expression (as would seem to be the way of all-out progressive education). We assume that they are already Christians, and we strive by our sensitive teaching to help them find their place *now* in the redemptive community, the Church.

If you wish a person to do well, you must provide the stimulus of recognition, the sense of distinction and selfhood among his companions. We must find for each child something he can do well. The child who may never find readiness in speech may find deep satisfaction in other original actions. To invent and start these is one of the neglected arts of teaching. True, we have had handwork of all sorts, but it has seldom been really applicable to the lesson or to the child.

The frequent use of the word "dynamic" means simply that we recognize the hidden life force in each one and try to bring it to fruition. Not all were made for glib talking or skilled painting, carving, or designing. Some can act, some

145

sing, some dance or be leaders. But all have the gift of praise. To be led to use this in the approach to God is the first level of religious teaching. Every child needs a friend and coach to start him being himself toward God.

42

The Art of Communication

"COMMUNICATION" is the word in education today. To *get through* a message from those in distress to those who can help is a problem that exists everywhere in human relations. People need help—generally only the simple support of human understanding, companionship, and acceptance. Yet they do not know how to ask for it, nor where. In their clumsy reaching-out their need is not recognized, or they are misunderstood. If those around them only knew, ready help would be given abundantly.

There are two parties to all communication—those who first signal, and those who should receive the message. Yet in the opportunities afforded by our living together, we may go on for years touching superficially, while our real selves never meet. This is the tragedy of many a classroom: there is seeming communication between teacher and pupils, but little meeting of minds.

A few intimates may arrive at a silent understanding, but most human beings conduct their relations by means of conversation. The medium of language is the normal and most common method of the meeting of persons. If you can't say what you mean, you cannot readily communicate with another. True, facial expressions, feelings revealed by actions, and the wordless reaching-out of sympathetic souls create a rich background. But always *words* are the main lines of communication.

Skill in the use of language is therefore necessary if persons are to profit by being together. We must know increasingly what to say and how and when to say it. We are now realizing the vast importance of all this in the art of teaching. Some teachers, for all their words, are not heard, inwardly or profitably, by the children. They are simply sounding off —the assigned story, preachment, drill, or lore.

Once genuine contact is established, communication is a two-way movement, an alternation of giving and receiving. This is what we recognize in the expression "give-and-take." Pupils have their part to give. Indeed, the teacher is outvoted at the very start—perhaps eight or ten to one—if he does not recognize that what his pupils are—what they are thinking and have experienced—is the raw material of learning.

How do we communicate with others? By striving earnestly to have our minds and spirits truly meet. Desiring this and knowing our failures in the past, we stop trusting in the old motives and ammunition of the classroom. We invite signals, we devise ways of answering them.

This has been going on gradually for a long time, but the new courses require and help us to sharpen our skills in human intercourse. Lesson preparation is vastly different. Instead of organizing prescribed material to be sent out on his own wave length, the teacher now plans how profitably to carry on the coming hour of fellowship in the Church with beloved friends who are, through a school year, learning the Christian religion by being together.

Consider a difficult child who is "acting up" in class. He is signaling something, and a wise adult may learn to answer. He may be saying in his own fumbling way that he needs attention, or praise. Or it may be he needs worthy responsibilities, a job, and direction. In a word, he needs to be *saved*, helped toward being the person God intended him to be.

We teachers must be so wholly alive to the realities of the Faith that we can communicate *ourselves* to other human beings. This is not merely the cliché, "What you are speaks more loudly than what you say." It is not shallow sentiment. We can learn ways of practicing it without being self-conscious. It calls for effort and, particularly, for "a peculiar and paradoxical blend of self-suppression and self-assertion."

"Real life is meeting" we have learned to say in our day. Many teachers, floundering a little between the old and the new, have found rare moments of success when, having given themselves and having been accepted, they felt that they were, for a single deep moment, at one with their pupils. This was made possible because the children realized that they were free to venture on their own, and so to be persons encountering the vital person of their teacher.

Dialogue is the medium of our meeting—a skillful use of language to share knowledge, feelings, and experience. But words between persons who are sincerely trying to meet pass into the deeper levels of unspoken understanding. This can happen to you next Sunday morning in your class, if love and trust prevail. When persons meet persons and intermingle, this is communion.

Is this too remote and too difficult for us teachers? We are saying only that the Christian religion is a life of companionship under which persons of all conditions meet in a common life. That life is Christ.

We now speak of this process of human contacts—so close, so completely touching that, as on electric wires, power may flow—as communication. But we have always known it as communion, one with another. That is why we come and go to the altar *together*. In that spirit may we all meet our pupils next Sunday, resolved to meet not only their bodies but their spirits.

A Closing Caution

As WE said at the start, this is a book for beginners. It should help those who feel drawn to teaching, but who are confused about the modern methods. It is designed also to help the teacher who, although he has been teaching for some time, is a little stale and would welcome fresh ideas. He wants to know what they are doing in other places. He has heard of other goals today, but as yet the fresh tides in Christian education have not touched the shores of his parish. The foregoing may have given him some of the forms and terms. With these he may begin to feel familiar.

But this book can scarcely have given the substance. We recall a comic series in our daily paper years ago, in which a character known as "Book-taught Bilkins" attempted confidently each day some new job or sport, his only preparation being that he had read about it in a book. His failures might well be yours. We therefore close with this grave caution:

There is not enough in this book to set you up in business. You will have to do some more reading. You will have to attend some meetings and take some instruction. You must see some of these things being done in real classes. Comparing notes with others engaged in these ways will help; none has arrived, each is on his own way. We are sure that if anyone attempted to carry out these suggestions *alone,* he would risk failure and frustration.

If you are now determined to teach, you will take this risk. Then, within the vigorous life of the Church, with the help of the Holy Spirit, you will *learn by teaching*.